CREDO IN UNUM DEUM

A STANCE AGAINST CHANCE

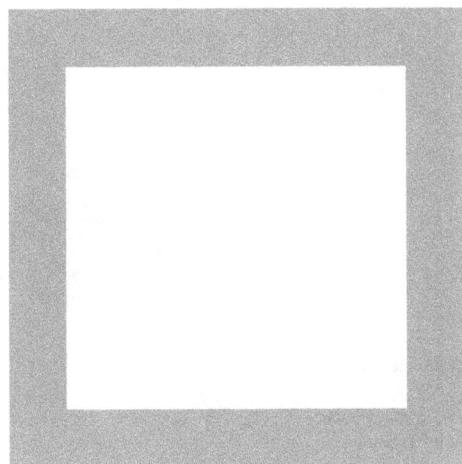

STEVE CHMIELEWSKI

CONTENTS

...

ACKNOWLEDGEMENTS

To not exist for yourself is a beautiful thing.

MIKE MCDANIEL

J esus let us know that the two most important commandments are to love God above all things and to love your neighbor. As a kid, I remember reading Gale Sayers's book, *I Am Third.* Here was a guy I looked up to as an athlete, and the fact that he put God first in his life was very intriguing to me at that time. Despite my admiration for him, it was difficult for me to latch onto the concept of putting others ahead of myself. That changed once I got married and had a family. Kara, Tom, Jamie, and Sydney, each in your own way, you made me want to be a better person, and you all made me realize what it means to care about someone more than I care about myself. Hopefully, because of each of you, I've made some progress on putting the well-being of others ahead of myself.

For me it's easier to write things than to say them, so I wrote this book with the hope you will always know how much I love you all, and that the only reason you are second is because when God is first the rest takes care of itself.

PREFACE

In heaven, there are going to be two lines, the long line and the short line, and I'm interested in being in the short line.

DENZEL WASHINGTON

I am a deeply flawed person, and anyone who knows me can read-ily attest to that. Let me be clear: I am not writing a book on "how to" live life as a Christian life. This book is intended to answer the question of *why* you should live life as a Christian. I think once you know the why, then the how becomes a priority. While the how may be a priority, for some of us it still is a challenge, but the why makes us keep trying.

I have often rationalized that if I could discount God or the Bible, in whole or part, then I could justify picking and choosing which of His teachings suited me. The "Cafeteria Christian" approach, if you will. Somewhere along the line, I concluded that He is who He says He is, and I better try harder to follow His ways and stop lying to myself when it's convenient to do so. I am passing along what I know to be true with the hope that it helps someone else. If there were some cosmic grab bag from which we each pulled our trials and tribulations, there's no way I would voluntarily put my hand back in the bag to try for a better deal, since I have had a very fortunate life. With that said, it is important to keep in mind that the trials and tribulations that come with life will never stop. But tests become much less stressful when you have Someone by your side who has all the answers.

God has never spoken to me audibly, and that is somewhat of a relief because the people to whom He does talk directly usually get put to the most difficult tests. I try to spend a significant amount of time thinking about God and praying about things I should be doing to serve Him. I enjoy writing, and after completing my last book, I was thinking about what I should write next. While going down a particular rabbit hole about Christianity, I came across *A short Schem on the True Religion* by Sir Isaac Newton. Since I have been called "S. Chem" in some manner for my entire life, it seemed like a signpost pointing me in the direction for my next book. Given that writing is a hobby, I have historically been very loose with timelines for completing books. Once I decided to write this book, I made a commitment to put aside other projects. I knew finishing this book would be a challenge because I knew that when it was finished, I would not only have to engage an editor but also a science editor, and I had no idea how to go about that. I was initially aiming for a 2024 release, since publishing one book a year seemed like a nice tidy timeline for me going forward. However, as 2024 was coming to a close, there was still a lot of wood left to chop. When I realized that 2025 would be the 1,700th anniversary of the Council of Nicaea, it seemed obvious as to when I should publish.

I need to make a full disclosure: Take everything I say for what it is—the opinion of one man, who is *not* claiming to be speaking in the name of God (Deuteronomy 18:20). Thus says Steve Chem, not the Lord. But I figured it would be a worthwhile project to articulate why I believe in God. If you think I'm full of beans, that's fine, but at least Ezekiel shouldn't be mad at me for trying (Ezekiel 33:9). If I'm wrong, the only thing I've lost was some time.

While faith in God is important on its own, God has given us plenty of tangible evidence to reinforce our faith. Throughout the ages, there has been a plethora of brilliant Christians who have created highly compelling content that dismantles the atheists' arguments and proves the veracity of God and the Christian faith. They are all more learned and greater thinkers than I, and they can expound in great depth upon all the topics herein. We are fortunate to have many current scholars who are keeping up with this great tradition of Christianity, and I highly recommend taking a deep dive into their works. I can't speak highly enough of the content produced by Stephen Meyer, James Tour, Michael Behe, Doug Axe, Michael Egnor, Joe Marino, Barry Schwartz, Jason Lisle, Rick Larson, Tim Mahoney, Thomas Purifoy, Jr., Andrew Snelling, Lee Strobel, Colin Humphreys, John Lennox, Gary Habermas, Frank Turek, William Dembski, Bryan Windle, Warner Wallace, and Charlie Campbell, to name a few. The real work has been done by these people who have spent a lifetime on each of these subjects. Meanwhile, I have curated, borrowed, and tried to distill from the best materials I am aware of on the subjects I cover. Often the arguments on these topics are recycled and the original source is not always clear, so it is unintentional if I did not cite someone, and please forgive me if I have made that mistake. Very little in here do I think could be originally attributed to me; I'm more of a mental midget standing on the shoulders of giants (hat tip to Sir Isaac Newton).

I have enormous respect for the people who dedicate themselves to scientific discovery, but it seems to me that too often the big picture gets overlooked. In the quantum world, a cat can be both dead and alive. As true as that may be, that is not what we experience in our everyday lives. When I think of the parable of the blind men and the elephant, it strikes me that the men were like atheist scientists working in their specific disciplines. Although they may be experts in their respective disciplines, their hyper-specialization blinds them from making connections between disciplines. Moreover, a too-common dogmatic adherence to an atheistic worldview further blinds experts and results in a fervent form of paganism. This problem undermines the role of science and education, which is to discover the truth and produce knowledge. Unfortunately, too many people take the word of these narrowly focused experts at face value rather than just looking at the elephant in the room.

God created a loop of complex systems within complex systems. I agree with Pascal's argument for the wager, but for me, there is enough evidence in many separate disciplines to convince me that God is who He says He is, and when you add up all the evidence across all disciplines, it's truly overwhelming. So in my view, there's no need to hedge with a wager. Following the instructions in 1 Peter 3:15 and Colossians 4:6, I've set out to write a pithy 360-degree examination of the evidence compiled from many different disciplines to explain why I confidently believe in God. This is a common-sense and big-picture view that is not meant to engage pettifoggers.

As I read the news each day, I have become leery when reading how major new scientific discoveries are reported. These discoveries are often hyped by the media as revolutionary and definitive, when in reality they usually result in more questions than answers. Because

I have presented discussions relating to the various sciences, history, and archeology, this book will always run the risk of being out of date. There is also the possibility that a scientific discovery obviates conclusions that have been reached herein. The fear of being wrong shouldn't scare us off from seeking answers. The pursuit of knowledge is humbling because only once we start to learn do we realize how little we know. We must be humble enough to admit that there are a lot of things we just don't know and probably never will in this lifetime. Materialists rarely show any signs of regret or embarrassment when new discoveries undermine their theories—it's just on to the next theory. On the other hand, a believer should not feel any shame for having to rework truly Bible-based theories and models to explain the new findings because we can take the long view, knowing that God is real and that eventually everything will be brought to light (Luke 8:17).

INTRODUCTION

He who thinks half-heartedly will not believe in God;
but he who really thinks has to believe in God.

SIR ISAAC NEWTON

As I lay out the many reasons why you should believe in the God of the Bible, you will see that I am presenting the material from the point of view that it is all true. I understand that this approach may be off-putting to those who are unsure or disagree with the premise. One of their critiques will be that my logic is circular because I keep using my belief that something is true to prove that something else is true. Augustine said that one must believe in God before one can understand. Let me put that a little differently for the modern sensibility. If I were to tell you that Roger Kint is Keyser Söze, that Tom Farrell is Yuri, and that Einhorn is Finkle before you watch the movies, you would have a very different experience than if I did not tell you. So, I am telling you that God is real and that the Bible is true before we get started so everything will make more sense as we proceed.

My road to believing was a mostly straight one. I was born into a Catholic family. I attended religious education and church every week. As a kid, practicing the faith always seemed like a chore: something I had to do, not something I wanted to do. There's a common argument that attempts to undermine believers in God who were raised in religious families. I give some credence to that argument because some people are certainly indoctrinated into religions at an impressionable age. On the other hand, I've come to realize that the more you are exposed to God, the more opportunity you will have to receive His grace and become a believer. Regardless of my religious upbringing, it's just not in my nature to buy into someone's baloney. I may not be from Missouri, but you still have to show me before I believe something. All of which is consistent with Paul telling us to "test everything; retain what is good" (1 Thessalonians 5:21).

Words are important, especially when debating. Certain words like *apologist* and *meek* tend to be misunderstood in religious contexts. I tend to avoid the word *apologist,* because it's misunderstood to mean the person is sorry about something. Even its actual meaning doesn't sit right with me as someone who is a defender of Christianity, because I like to think I am meek enough to know that God doesn't need me or anyone to defend Him. As I got older and became more intellectually curious, I became more cognizant of atheists and their arguments, so I started looking at how to debunk various atheists' arguments. At first, I tended to agree with Jeff Allen's observation, "You are not an atheist, you are a moron." But I realized it's important to listen and understand their arguments (Proverbs 18:13). While I have often wondered if they are unwilling or truly incapable of believing, we know it must be the former, because God rejoices over the salvation of just one sinner (Luke 15:7). I try to keep that opportunity in mind when debating with someone, so I remain respectful with the hope that maybe I can make a breakthrough. It's human nature to dig in during a debate, and it's extremely hard for most people to admit when they are wrong. I find it incumbent on the believer to make it easy for the nonbeliever to come around and welcome them to the team. Be humble, because we are all sinners and all unworthy. Make it known that all it takes to receive God's forgiveness and acceptance is to simply say, "I believe" (see Matthew 9:28). That's a light burden and easy yoke if I ever saw one (Matthew 11:28). Also remember that we are called to forgive one another every time someone seeks it (Matthew 18:21–22). Remember, it's not the proud but the humble who will inherit the Earth (Matthew 5:5). Believe and be humble.

The key to debunking arguments is to break them down one at a time, piece by piece. I firmly believe that one should not live in an echo chamber and that being exposed to a diversity of views is an important part of learning. There are certainly many atheists with whom you can have respectful, pleasant conversations, and I am grateful to them. The challenge lies in dealing with the atheists who argue like progressives. They like to make what I call bumper sticker arguments: *War is bad.* Thanks, Captain Obvious! The fact of the matter is that sometimes war is necessary, and if you are ever in a position where you are trying to justify a war, you are not going to fit your argument on a bumper sticker or in a three-minute ditty. That challenge is even harder to overcome in today's Tik Tok-meme-tl;dr world. Moreover, comedy and the ability to embarrass, while being incapable of being embarrassed, are the superpowers of many an atheist. On the surface a lot of what Christians believe is incredulous, so it's easy to make fun of it. No one likes to get laughed at, so if someone makes a joke about Jesus raising Lazarus from the dead and the Christian doesn't laugh, the Christian is then left to answer the awkward question, "You actually believe that? And before the Christian can even get a word out in response, the next joke about water being turned into wine had already been piled on. A proper response requires time and presentation skills, which not a lot of people are willing to spend the time practicing. The lack of pithy coherent responses and, God forbid, humorous responses compounds the problem; movies like *Religulous* or the story of Banana Man (i.e., Ray Comfort) get ingrained in pop culture like a bad variant of the Mandela Effect. The irony here is that the more scientists learn about us and our world, the less they realize they know, but rarely will they admit it. Unfortunately, too many Christians turn tail back into the closet for fear of becoming fodder for the progressive, haughty, cocksure, intellectual, and pseudo-intellectual atheists with a certain degree of wit or stage presence. Peter called them scoffers and mockers (2 Peter 3:3). I like to call them cocksures.

Cocksures generally reject Christianity because God doesn't meet their expectations, which in turn results in the intellectual framework that allows them to be their own gods with their own moral code. This is one of the traps of hubris, as G. K. Chesterton noted: "When men choose not to believe in God, they do not thereafter believe in nothing, they then become capable of believing in anything."[1] While that worldview may appear empowering, the intellectual framework is enfeebling, since they have no real power other than the power to criticize. Ironically, they gain stature by criticizing the One who created all things visible and invisible. They do so with a false sense of immunity because, as their thinking goes, if God is so great, why doesn't *He* answer their critiques? But He has, long ago. You can find His answer in the rhetorical questions and undressing He put to Job

---

1. G. K. Chesterton, "Quotable Quote," Goodreads, https://www.goodreads.com/quotes/44015-when-men-choose-not-to-believe-in-god-they-do (accessed January 30, 2025).

(Job 38). To anyone who questions God, they should first answer this question posed to Job: "Where were you when I laid the foundations of the Earth?" (verse 4 NKJV). He reiterated this to Isaiah when He said, "As the heavens are higher than the Earth, so are my ways higher than your ways, my thoughts higher than your thoughts" (Isaiah 55:9). If you don't understand the world you live in, what makes you think you can understand the reasoning of the One who created it? Cocksures have no answer to this question, and because they are not burdened with humility, they simply ignore the One who asks it and pretend He doesn't exist.

Cocksures say silly things, like religion is only able to propagate because it is never questioned or criticized, and believers live in an echo chamber. This is particularly rich given that cocksures dominate academia, which has become one of the most secularized and insular closed-minded groups you will find. They can spread their views unabated through their favored media outlets, which hold similar world views. It's hard to quantify the scientific discoveries that have been stifled because of this stubbornness. You know these people by the code phrases they use like "settled science." But science is never settled, nor does it hold an opinion. It is the *scientific method* that is important, because that's the tool to be used to better understand things.

Cocksures often seem upset the Bible doesn't contain the insights, morality, or inventions that *they* want, and thus they view it as cruel and rudimentary. They think that the Bible is not something that a divine Creator would bestow and that it should not be considered moral or holy because of all these perceived faults. It's simply too simple for the learned. But that is probably a feature, not a bug. I always struggled with the Old Testament, because so many of the events are so incredible and were written so long ago that it seemed more likely to me that these stories were fictionalized or were meant as parables. When asked about the Old Testament stories, I would say something to this effect: "I believe in God, but not *those* things." Cocksures exploit this insecurity by saying things like the Bible is fraudulent because it gets pi wrong. Some context is needed to refute that view. Pi is an amazing number. I will discuss math more later, but suffice it to say that God could send you on a lifelong journey studying pi. It is an irrational number, meaning that it has an infinite amount of numbers after the decimal point that will never repeat. Consider what it was like for the first person to realize that the sequence 79873884 occurs four times in the first 200 million digits of pi, and the second time it does, it occurs exactly at position 79813884 (when counting from the first digit after the decimal point). Now, consider a God who knows all this but decided to condescend to His audience for a particular situation. The various books of the Bible were written to meet people where they were at that time. If you are talking about pi to Homer Simpson, you should realize he is probably thinking about pie—floor pie. If you are talking to NASA engineers, you should be prepared to go out to fifteen decimal places. If you want to calculate the circumference of a circle the size of the visible universe down to the width of one hydrogen atom, then 38 decimal places suffices.[2] However, if you are talking to people in the fifth or sixth century BC, you might simply round pi to 3, because it's close enough without being tedious for that context (1 Kings 7:23–26; 2 Chronicles 4:2–5).

Why doesn't the Bible say anything about harnessing electricity, DNA, or how to cure cancer? I don't know, but the Book says, and it logically follows, that His foolishness is wiser than human wisdom.

---

2. Numberphile, "Pi and the Size of the Universe," YouTube, February 20, 2013, www.youtube.com/watch?v=FpyrF_Ci2TQ (accessed January 22, 2025).

What I do know is that it is brazenly arrogant to question the One who named all the stars and put them in their places, while being in awe of the Las Vegas Sphere. After God created the world, Adam and Eve had all they needed. He gave them a couple of simple rules, and they couldn't get those right. Maybe He decided that if we don't want to listen, then He would let us figure things out the hard way. It's obvious that God created a discoverable universe, and He watches us try to figure things out for ourselves over time. I like to think of these clues as the ultimate Easter eggs. Daniel LaRusso didn't understand why he was waxing cars, but there was a reason to it that he didn't understand, yet someone with greater wisdom did. Every parent knows the joy of watching their kids figure something out on their own. There are lots of questions we don't have the answer to, and that's all right because discovery and exploration are exciting, and we have been promised that someday all will be revealed (Luke 8:17). Just because we don't know everything today doesn't mean we should be defensive when cocksures mock knowledge gaps and attempt to dismiss the overwhelming evidence for God by citing the God of the gaps fallacy. The gaps will be filled in His time, but in the meantime, God has already revealed more than enough for us to know that He is who He says He is.

The turning point for me came after I more closely examined what Jesus was doing and saying in the New Testament. The Old and New Testaments play off each other like different acts in a play, and once I understood that Jesus was the fulfillment of the Old Testament, the whole play made sense. Jesus authenticated the story of creation when He stated, "From the beginning the Creator 'made them male and female' " (Matthew 19:4). Jesus also specifically corroborated some of the more fantastic stories in the Old Testament such as Noah (Matthew 24:37–39), Lot (Luke 17:28), and Jonah

(Matthew 12:40). At the beginning of His ministry, in Luke 4:21, He said that He was fulfilling the Scripture written by Isaiah (Isaiah 61:1). These are just a few of the many examples of Jesus validating the Old Testament. There is no way to read the New Testament without concluding that Jesus attested that the Old Testament is the holy and authentic Word of God. That is why the cocksures *must* attack Jesus. He knew this would be the case, so He prepared His followers so that they would know that it would be hard to convince some people because no matter how much evidence there is, some people are never going to believe in Him (2 Peter 3:3–4).

Some cocksures dismiss the God of the Bible because the Judeo-Christian teachings are built on fear of the Lord, but that too is a feature, not a bug. Fear of God is the beginning of wisdom (Proverbs 9:10). For anyone with kids, you know what it feels like to tell them not to do something that may cause them harm. You do this because you are looking out for their best interest, yet there are times when they will look at you as if you are their enemy because they don't have the wisdom you do. We are all God's children, and it is no different with us. God forbade Adam and Eve from eating from the Tree of the Knowledge of Good and Evil because He knew this would be bad for mankind, perhaps because knowledge without wisdom is deadly. It's difficult to hear many of the things Jesus said. He told us that following Him may cause others to hate you for it. Believing in Him may also split families (Matthew 10:21–22). It's hard when someone asks whether you actually believe that a loving God would want families to be torn apart. That; however, is a misleading question. Jesus *doesn't want* families to be torn apart; He *wants* people to exercise their free will and believe in Him so they can gain eternal life (John 3:36). He recognizes that not everyone will do so, and sadly, the result is division, even in families. He doesn't want you to give up easily on those relationships. He tells us not only to love and forgive but also to stay true to Him, and remember, if you do give up something for Him, you will be repaid (Matthew 19:29). Listen to Him and trust Him.

Another sleight of hand used to undermine Christianity is lumping it in with all other "religions." This trick usually starts with getting the believer to admit that they reject all gods but Him, as if there is something intellectually inconsistent about that. There are an infinite number of wrong answers to a lot of questions. For instance, I reject all solutions but 4 as the answer to the question, "What is 2 + 2?" There is nothing intellectually inconsistent about rejecting all other "gods" but the one true God of the Bible. For that reason, I am not going to spend time debunking other religions. The God of the Bible has clearly stated, "I am the LORD, there is no other" (Isaiah 45:5) and Jesus said, "The Father and I are one" (John 10:30), and that "No one comes to the Father except through Me" (John 14:6). Once we prove that the Father, Son, and the Holy Spirit are who They say They are, it eliminates the hassle of debunking all of the other religions. Even most of the cocksures admit that no serious person denies Jesus existed, so we are now faced with C.S. Lewis' insightful observation that Jesus must be either a liar, lunatic, or Lord. The really good news is that once you have the confidence to believe that Jesus is who He says He is, you can take *everything* in the Bible at face value—you are in for a penny, in for a pound. This is particularly helpful when something in the Bible seems too implausible or contradictory to what you think you know or what others say must be so. Just retrace your steps on the trail of logic that led you to believe in the first place: Jesus is who He says He is, He and the Father are One, there is no other god, and the Bible is the Word of God. It's that simple.

Cocksures like to paint Christians as deniers and obstruction-
ists of science, and there certainly are egregious examples they can
point to throughout history. But the truth of the matter is that by
and large, Christians have always been in the forefront of searching
for answers and conducting scientific discovery. Nonetheless, it's a
good thing that science is not controlled by a church because oppos-
ing views should always be welcome. The good news for believers
is that the more sophisticated science gets, the more evidence there
is for a Creator. This has put the cocksures on the defensive. Christians can investigate the Universe with confidence, and when science appears to be in conflict with the Bible, they know they ought
to pause. Perhaps the science isn't good, or perhaps the portion of
the Bible needs to be reinterpreted. The secularist scientist is forced
to reject the creationist view out of hand. Their flat-out unwilling-
ness to be open to debate and alternate theories is bad for the progress of science.

I have spent a lot of time looking for proof that backs up what I
believe. This has prompted me to ask questions: What do I believe,
and why? The Nicene Creed provides a beautiful synopsis of what
Christians believe, and by extension, it provides a road map for the
proof we should look for to support our beliefs. The Creed acknowl-
edges that God is the maker of Heaven and Earth, of all things visible and invisible. By using the Creed as your testament, a believer can
parry the cocksure who mocks the fact that there are many forms of
Christianity and that it is practiced in many ways, some of which are
no doubt heretical. Don't be hesitant to acknowledge that churches
are institutions run by man and are always susceptible to becoming
corrupt. One analogy I can think of is that I believe that the United
States Constitution is an amazing foundation for a democratic republic

form of government, but I doubt there are many amongst us who wouldn't say that our current government and politicians are less than to be desired. Other democracies are even worse. That is why one must follow principles, not people. The same holds true for Christianity. More on this later.

Even the Creed itself was not accepted by all those who were involved in drafting it. The Creed was originally written in Greek and would be later translated into Latin. If you want a Christian history rabbit hole to go down, look up how the addition of the word *filioque* to the Creed caused a major split between the Catholic and Eastern churches. The problem with translating texts, religious or otherwise, is that it stirs up endless debate, so I have come to appreciate the wisdom of the Catholic Church's continued use of Latin. The language is frozen in time, thus making it impervious to change, which is important for relaying the truth across generations. You can end up going round and round the merry-go-round, arguing about anything and everything related to Christianity. In my own faith, I had to find a starting point, and that is the Creed, because it captures Christianity's core beliefs. In my view, everything else is lesser important details to be explored and debated in good faith, but not to be used for division amongst Christians.

Here's the Creed in Latin from the singular perspective (as opposed to the plural *CREDIMUS*), with one version of an English translation.

CREDO IN UNUM DEUM, PATREM OMNIPO-TENTEM, FACTOREM CAELI ET TERRAE, VISIBIL-IUM OMNIUM ET INVISIBILIUM.

I believe in one God, the Father almighty, maker of Heaven and Earth, of all things visible and invisible.

ET IN UNUM DOMINUM IESUM CHRISTUM, FIL-IUM DEI UNIGENITUM, EX PATRE NATUM, ANTE OMNIA SAECULA. DEUM DE DEO, LUMEN DE LUMINE, DEUM VERUM DE DEO VERO, GENITUM NON FACTUM, CONSUBSTANTIALEM PATRI; PER QUEM OMNIA FACTA SUNT.

And in one Lord, Jesus Christ, the only-begotten Son of God, born of the Father before all ages. God from God, Light from Light, true God from true God, begotten, not made, consubstantial with the Father; through Whom all things were made.

QUI PROPTER NOS HOMINES ET PROPTER NOS-TRAM SALUTEM DESCENDIT DE CAELIS. ET INCARNATUS EST DE SPIRITU SANCTO EX MARIA VIRGINE, ET HOMO FACTUS EST.

Who for us men and for our salvation came down from Heaven. And He was made flesh by the Holy Spirit from the Virgin Mary, and was made man.

CRUCIFIXUS ETIAM PRO NOBIS SUB PONTIO PILATO, PASSUS ET SEPULTUS EST, ET RESURREXIT TERTIA DIE, SECUNDUM SCRIPTURAS, ET ASCEN-DIT IN CAELUM, SEDET AD DEXTERAM PATRIS.

He was crucified for us under Pontius Pilate; suffered, and was buried. On the third day He rose again according to the Scriptures; He ascended into Heaven and sits at the right hand of the Father.

ET ITERUM VENTURUS EST CUM GLORIA, IUDI-CARE VIVOS ET MORTUOS, CUIUS REGNI NON ERIT FINIS.

He will come again in glory to judge the living and the dead, and His kingdom will have no end.

ET IN SPIRITUM SANCTUM, DOMINUM ET VIVIF-ICANTEM, QUI EX PATRE FILIOQUE PROCEDIT.

And [I believe] in the Holy Spirit, the Lord and giver of life, Who proceeds from the Father and the Son.

QUI CUM PATRE ET FILIO SIMUL ADORATUR ET CONGLORIFICATUR: QUI LOCUTUS EST PER PROPHETAS.

Who, with the Father and the Son, is adored and glorified: Who has spoken through the Prophets.

ET UNAM, SANCTAM, CATHOLICAM ET APOS-TOLICAM ECCLESIAM.

And (I believe in) one holy, catholic and apostolic Church.

CONFITEOR UNUM BAPTISMA IN REMISSIONEM PECCATORUM. ET EXPECTO RESURRECTIONEM MORTUORUM, ET VITAM VENTURI SAECULI. AMEN.

I confess one baptism for the remission of sins. And I look for the resurrection of the dead, and the life of the age to come. Amen.

It's hard to decide on a launching point from which I should begin laying the evidence that supports the Creed being true. There are innumerable points to make, with some being more obvious and intuitive than others. I am going to take some selected pieces of evidence and put them together like a giant jigsaw puzzle. As I put the pieces together, the big picture will become clear to different people at different times. The first thing I suggest you do is to watch a short video called "Cosmic Eye,"[3] which zooms in on elementary particles and zooms out to the cosmos. This ought to put you in the right frame of mind to appreciate the loop of complex systems within complex systems that God has created.

I have decided to present the evidence in a way that parallels the Trinity. When I think of God the Father, I think of the evidence of the Creation and the resulting immutable laws that exist not only as immaterial concepts but also as laws that govern the physical world. When I think of Jesus, I think of God becoming man and leaving behind a historical record from His time on Earth. When I think of the Holy Spirit, I think of the spiritual evidence that we all experience in our souls.

---

3. Scientificus, "Universe Size Comparison: Cosmic Eye," YouTube, April 30, 2018, https://www.youtube.com/watch?v=8Are9dDbW24 (accessed January 23, 2025).

PART I

PATER

I believe in one God, the
Father almighty, maker of
Heaven and Earth, of all
things visible and invisible.

In all chaos there is a cosmos, in all disorder a secret order.

CARL GUSTAV JUNG

A theists historically have taken up Aristotle's view that the Universe is eternal. While the number is constantly changing, and there is no definitive proof, the current consensus estimate from secular scientists for the age of the Universe is approximately 13.8 billion years. Edwin Hubble is credited for observing that the Universe is expanding, although no one has the foggiest idea what it is expanding into. If the Universe is expanding, then secularists are forced to admit that if you were to go backward in time, the Universe would be smaller and smaller until at some point the Universe was a single point from which it began—that is, what the secularists call the Big Bang.

The more we learn, the more problems arise for secularists' timelines and theories. The James Webb Space Telescope (JWST) continues to confound secularists because there are so many fully formed galaxies further and further away from us, despite their models predicting that these galaxies would be unevolved. Secularists' models for the Universe's evolution are undermined by the fact that it is now observed that the Universe is expanding faster than they expect.[4] This has been coined as the "Hubble Tension" since this "constant" appears to be in flux according to the JWST's confirmation of the Hubble Telescope's measurements of the Cepheid variable stars.[5] What's a secularist to do? One option is to employ a theory that adds or subtracts "dark energy" which has never been observed. Another option is to circle back to their old friend: time. Secularists' "new" theories often require them to monkey with time, usually by adding some, but sometimes new data forces them to remove some. Ten years ago, NASA claimed that the first stars were formed 400 million years after the Big Bang, and the most recent estimate is 250 million years after the Big Bang. What's 150 million years between friends? And then there is the recent theory that the Universe is now twice as old because light gets tired.[6] Always be on the lookout for the secularists' sleight of hand trick with time. When they can't make sense of something, they monkey with time to "fix" the problem. One of the hardest things for humans to do is admit they are wrong. What's easier, admitting you are wrong or adding or subtracting billions or millions of years to the age of the Universe?

In 2021, the Giant Arc in the sky was discovered, and it is 3.3 billion light-years across. In 2024, a second mysterious ultra-large

4. Johns Hopkins University, "Universe Expansion Study Confirms Challenge to Cosmic Theory," Science Daily, December 9, 2024, https://www.sciencedaily.com/releases/2024/12/241209122620.htm (accessed January 23, 2025).

5. Adam G. Riess, et al., "JWST Observations Reject Unrecognized Crowding of Cepheid Photometry as an Explanation for the Hubble Tension at 8σ Confidence," The Astrophysical Journal Letters, vol. 962, no 1 (February 6, 2024), https://iopscience.iop.org/article/10.3847/2041-8213/ad1ddd (accessed January 23, 2025).

6. "The Universe Could Be Twice as Old If Light Is Tired and Physical Constants Change," Universe Today, https://www.universetoday.com/162394/the-universe-could-be-twice-as-old-if-light-is-tired-and-physical-constants-change/#:~:text=In%20the%20tired%20light%20model,reddening%20of%20light%20over%20time (accessed January 23, 2025).

structure, known as the Big Ring on the sky, was discovered. It has a diameter of approximately 1.3 billion light-years and is about 9.2 billion light-years away from Earth. These structures appear to breach what cosmologists deem to be theoretically possible because they are too big.[78] The nearby galaxy called J0613+52, defies the typical characteristics of galaxies because it appears to consist of primordial gas. The dwarf galaxy called Nube[9] undermines the "settled science" relating to dark matter, which, again, has never been observed, but it serendipitously balanced Einstein's equation for special relativity, despite the fact that he did not know what dark matter was.

The point being made here is not that secular scientists ought to be mocked for being wrong; rather, the cocksures ought to be mocked for being consistently wrong with zero reputational impact, all the while having the gall to claim that they are the science settlers. Einstein, apparently no theist, at least had the humility to admit that "the human mind, no matter how highly trained, cannot grasp the Universe. We are in the position of a little child, entering a huge library whose walls are covered to the ceiling with books in many different tongues. The child knows that someone must have written those books. It does not know who or how. It does not understand the languages in which they are written. The child notes a definite plan in the arrangement of the books, a mysterious order,

7. DES Collaboration, "The Dark Energy Survey: Cosmology Results With ~1500 New High-red-shift Type Ia Supernovae Using the Full 5-Year Dataset," Arxiv.org, March 29, 2024, https://arxiv.org/abs/2401.02929 (accessed January 23, 2025).

8. "Discovery of a Giant Arc in Distant Space Adds to Challenges to Basic Assumptions about the Universe," University of Central Lancashire, June 7, 2021, https://www.uclan.ac.uk/news/discovery-of-a-giant-arc-in-distant-space-adds-to-challenges-to-basic-assumptions-about-the-universe (accessed January 23, 2025).

9. Mireia Montes, et al., "An Almost Dark Galaxy with the Mass of the Small Magellanic Cloud," Astronomy & Astrophysics, vol. 681 (January 2024), https://www.aanda.org/articles/aa/full_html/2024/01/aa47667-23/aa47667-23.html (accessed January 23, 2025).

which it does not comprehend, but only dimly suspects."[10] Werner Heisenberg had a slightly different take when he said, "Not only is the Universe stranger than we think, it is stranger than we can think."[11] One astronomer who recently observed the JWST data said, "We need to find out if we are missing something on how to connect the beginning of the Universe to the present day." How about God? The Universe is stranger than we can think, because we do not think like God.

Secular scientists' starting point for the Universe is the Big Bang, whereas the Bible tells us very clearly what happened in the beginning. The Bible doesn't say how old the Earth is. This omission leads to a lot of debate amongst Bible believers as to whether the first days were actual twenty-four-hour days or some longer period. While God could certainly calculate time using oscillations of cesium atoms, the units of time He set forth for us are the day, the week, and the year. Unfortunately, the first couple of days are a quandary because the Sun wasn't created until the fourth day, so it's hard to reconcile this with our concept of a day, or of a year for that matter, which are defined by relative movements of the Earth and Sun. Amongst creationists there is this tension between Old Earthers (the initial days were longer than twenty-four hours) and Young Earthers (the initial days were twenty-four hours long). To me it looks like the Old Earthers didn't much like being mocked by the scoffers, so they came up with a theory that is compatible with the "settled science."

The beginning of time and the Universe is probably not meaningful in any sort of temporal sense that our limited minds can comprehend,

---

10. Albert Einstein, "Quotable Quote," Goodreads, https://www.goodreads.com/quotes/263668-your-question-is-the-most-difficult-in-the-world-it (accessed January 30, 2025).

11. Werner Heisenberg, "Quotable Quote," Goodreads, https://www.goodreads.com/quotes/164668-not-only-is-the-universe-stranger-than-we-think-it (accessed January 30, 2025).

because one day with the Lord is like a thousand years, and a thousand years like one day (2 Peter 3:8). The concept of time during Creation week is also difficult to comprehend, and as TV's greatest private investigator found out, time has little to do with infinity and jelly doughnuts. Nonetheless, in the inconceivably brief first moments of the Universe's creation, an awful lot of "time" could have happened. God then created stars, planets, grown people, animals, and plants. All these things may have appeared to be "old" because they appeared to have some sort of history when they didn't (2 Peter 3:5). Time as we know it and experience it today seems to normalize over the course of that first week, so by the time God creates man on Day 6, time would be recognizable to us. So, the sobriquet "Young Earther" isn't accurate. I would suggest that it's a fool's errand arguing about exactly what happened during the week of Creation or what the Earth was even like prior to Noah's flood. The important takeaway is not how much "time" has passed since Creation week; the point that you should focus on is that *there was a Creation*. From nothing came something—everything!

At the end of Day 6 of Creation week, everything was in place and God rested. Everything in the physical world was in place, and it was all good. For everything that has ever been, it would have to have been in the most ordered state it has ever been in. This is consistent with the Second Law of Thermodynamics, which states that disorder, or entropy, always increases. Although God *could* intervene at any time, He no longer *needed* to, since the Universe was complete and the physical laws and constants were established to govern it. There should be no surprise when astronomers discover the ultra-large structure, since He tells us that although He has named them all, He created more stars than *we* could ever identify or number

(Genesis 15:5; 22:17; Deuteronomy 1:10; 10:22). Yet He created this special home for us.

It's inconceivably special when you consider how inconceivable the Universe is. The level of detail is inconceivable, but try considering just a few of the details: The Earth's distance from the Sun is just right for a stable water cycle. If the Earth were too close, water would boil; too far away, and it would freeze. Meanwhile, the Earth is designed to deflect 1.5 million tons of solar material each second.[12] The Earth's axial tilt, magnetic field, crust thickness, and amounts and proportions of oxygen, nitrogen and carbon dioxide are all perfectly set up to support our life on Earth. The Earth's relationship to the Moon stabilizes the Earth's orbit, rotation, and tides. On and on it goes. I understand G.K. Chesterton's point when he stated, "We should be startled by the sun, and not by the eclipse";[13] however, I think we should be startled by the precision of all of it. For a detailed discussion on just how special the Earth is and what a magnificent architect He is, I suggest *The Privileged Planet*, by Guillermo Gonzalez and Jay W. Richards.

Some atheists make the silly arguments that they don't believe in a Creator because there is no signature on His creation. On the contrary, His signature is everywhere: "The heavens declare the glory of God; the skies proclaim the work of His hands" (Psalm 19:1 NIV). His handiwork is laid out for us to appreciate and discover, and there are amazing stories from His handiwork told in the stars.

---

12. ORBITGEO, "Each Second, Earth's Magnetic Field Deflects 1.5 Million Tons of Solar Material," YouTube, February 5, 2024, https://www.youtube.com/watch?v=fCd488WqZ0Y (accessed January 23, 2025).

13. G. K. Chesterton, "Quotable Quote," Goodreads, https://www.goodreads.com/quotes/98137-we-should-always-endeavor-to-wonder-at-the-permanent-thing (accessed January 30, 2025).

MATH

Math is conceptual. It exists beyond time and space and is independent of our minds. If all the math books that have ever been written were destroyed, math would still exist and could be rediscovered again. While math is conceptual, it is also orderly, predictable, universal, invariant, contains information, and explains things. All of the characteristics of math are necessary for life, because life could not exist if there was no order. Numbers themselves are abstract; they do not exist in the physical world. There are an infinite number of numbers as well as an infinite number of numbers between each number. Each number has its own individual properties that remain true, thus preventing you or me from giving pi some other value that you or I may want it to be.

Because math is universal, Ellie Arroway figured that something sending a repeating signal of beats and pauses signifying the sequence of prime numbers from 2 to 101 had to be intelligent. While it makes for good fiction to build a story around Ellie trying to figure out where the signal came from, as a matter of reality, a better story would be figuring out where math comes from. It must come from a mind, because math contains information. The information is conceptual, yet it controls our Universe; therefore, the source of this information has to be from outside of our Universe. Galileo summed it up nicely when he said, "Math is the language in which God has written the Universe." That statement is particularly profound, since math contains every possible combination of numbers; moreover, since math can be used as code for letters, then every sequence of letters exists in math. Thus, every book ever written or that could be written in this Universe exists within math.

For the sake of brevity, and because I am not exactly a candidate for the Vienna Circle, it is beyond the scope of this book to go into much detail about math. However, if you want to understand why Galileo was right, an interesting place to start is with the Fibonacci sequence. This is a sequence in which each number is the sum of the two preceding numbers (0, 1, 1, 2, 3, 5, 8, and so on). Then check out the Golden Ratio,[14] which is known by the Greek letter ϕ, and which is calculated as the ratio of $(a + b) / a$ = the ratio of a / b. It is equal to approximately 1.618. As abstractions, the Fibonacci sequence and Golden Ratio are interesting, in part because as the Fibonacci sequence progresses, the ratio of consecutive Fibonacci numbers converges to the Golden Ratio. However, what makes them *amazing* is their *application* to the physical Universe. The Golden Ratio becomes special in the physical Universe because it dictates a particular spatial relationship that is aesthetically pleasing and is thus fundamental throughout art (e.g., Da Vinci's Mona Lisa) and architecture (e.g., the Parthenon). More importantly, they are fundamental in nature. The Golden Ratio can be seen throughout the design of the human body (see Da Vinci's Vitruvian Man). It can even be seen in our skulls.[15] The Fibonacci sequence can be found everywhere in nature, from spiral galaxies to pinecone spirals and seed heads on sunflowers. Look at the petals on a flower, and you will see that the number aligns with its flower family (e.g., lilies and irises have three petals, buttercups have five petals, delphiniums have eight petals, marigolds have thirteen petals, and so on). It's undeniable that the physical Universe is affected by mathematical laws.

---

14. Gary Meisner, "Mathematics of Phi, 1.618, the Golden Number," Golden Number, May 16, 2012, https://www.goldennumber.net/math/ (accessed January 23, 2025).

15. Mike McRae, "The Golden Ratio Has Been Found in the Human Skull, But What Does It Mean?" Science Alert, October 4, 2019, https://www.sciencealert.com/the-golden-ratio-has-been-found-in-the-human-skull-but-exactly-what-does-it-mean (accessed January 23, 2025).

If your intellectual curiosity for more math has been piqued, I suggest watching Dr. Jason Lisle's presentation[16] regarding the Mandelbrot set. The Mandelbrot set is a set of complex numbers, one real and one imaginary, that is generated using the simple equation $Z = Z^2 + C$. A number (C) is input into the equation, and 0 is used as the starting point for Z. If Z stays small and does not grow infinitely, then that C is in the Mandelbrot set (e.g., −1 is in the set; 1 is not). When plotted on a plane with the X axis representing the real axis and the Y axis representing the imaginary axis, amazing patterns are revealed. Curiously, Fibonacci numbers are actually hidden within the Mandelbrot set. When you see the illustration, remember that these patterns are *not created*; they *just exist*, and they are infinite. Only Someone who is infinite can produce the infinite. The illustration of the Mandelbrot set gives you an opportunity to begin to understand what an infinite mind like God's is like. The simple nature of the equation and the binary aspect of the Mandelbrot set is worth contemplating, because a number is either in or not in. The numbers that are in the set are part of something infinite and beautiful. The numbers that are not in the set exist outside, in apparent nothingness. That reminds me of another binary set, and one for which I would like to be part of the "in" set (Matthew 3:12).

I will wrap up the math discussion with Kurt Gödel, who was an all-time great logician, mathematician, and philosopher. His Incompleteness Theorem concludes, much to the despair of atheists, that there are truths within any mathematical system that cannot be proven by the system. This is partly because mathematical laws exist outside

---

16. Indian Hills Community Church, "The Secret Code of Creation—Dr. Jason Lisle," YouTube, February 22, 2019, https://www.youtube.com/watch?v=kEyPWJVYp84&t=442s (accessed January 23, 2025).

of our system, meaning our Universe, and thus they require a Law-giver. I believe in the Lawgiver. For the nonbelievers, I refer you to Yogi who more simply and astutely observed, "You're not out of it until it's mathematical." Well, it's mathematical that God exists. If you want the proof, then check out Gödel's.[17]

Axiom 1: $\{P(\varphi) \land \Box\forall x[\varphi(x) \rightarrow \psi(x)]\} \rightarrow P(\psi)$

- If a positive property always causes another property, that second property must also be positive.

Axiom 2: $P(\neg\varphi) \leftrightarrow \neg P(\varphi)$

- A property is either positive or negative.

Theorem 1: $P(\varphi) \rightarrow \Diamond\exists x[\varphi(x)]$

- If a property is positive, then something can logically have that property (i.e., good things exist).

Definition 1: $G(x) \Leftrightarrow \forall\varphi[P(\varphi) \rightarrow \varphi(x)]$

- An entity is God-like if it has all positive properties.

Axiom 3: $P(G)$

- Being God-like is a positive property.

Theorem 2: $\Diamond \, \exists x \, G(x)$

- It is possible God exists.

Definition 2: $\varphi \text{ ess } x \Leftrightarrow \varphi(x) \land \forall\psi\{\psi(x) \rightarrow \Box\forall y[\varphi(y) \rightarrow \psi(y)]\}$

17. Robert J. Marks and Samuel Haug, "Gödel Says God Exists and Proves It," Mind Matters, June 7, 2021, https://mindmatters.ai/2021/06/godel-says-god-exists-and-proves-it/ (accessed January 23, 2025).

- A property P is the essence of an entity x if x has P and P is minimal, i.e., the essential property P must cause every other property that x has because no smaller set of properties defines x.

Axiom 4: $P(\varphi) \rightarrow \Box P(\varphi)$

- A positive property must be necessarily positive.

Theorem 3: $G(x) \rightarrow G\ ess\ x$

- Being God-like means having every positive property.

Definition 3: $E(x) \Leftrightarrow \forall\varphi[\varphi\ ess\ x \rightarrow \Box \exists y\ \varphi(y)]$

- An entity x necessarily exists if it has at least one essential property.

Axiom 5: $P(E)$

- Necessary existence (having at least one essential property) is a positive property, so existing is good.

Theorem 4: $\Box\ \exists x\ G(x)$

- It is necessary that there is an object x that is God-like, i.e., it is necessary that God exists.

PHYSICS

Physics also leaves us with two options regarding God's existence. I believe that God exists and created the Universe because His finely tuned design produced the initial conditions, fundamental forces, and fundamental constants without which our Universe could not exist. Scoffers believe in chance and a bunch of coincidences.

Consider the initial conditions at the Creation. The conditions were such that the density of matter and energy in the Universe was just precise enough that it did not collapse, nor did it expand too fast for galaxies, stars, and planets to exist. A mathematical physicist named Roger Penrose calculated the odds of this precision having occurred to be $10^{10^{123}}$.[18] There is no way for a human to comprehend this number; suffice it to say that you couldn't write all of those zeros in your lifetime. Another issue materialists have to solve for is known as the flatness problem.[19] Data show that the Universe is flat, while the expectation is that it should be curved. The probability of this flatness occurring is once again extremely low. Now consider that life as we know it is only possible because of carbon; however, ^{12}C is very hard to produce.[20] If the energy level of the ^{12}C nucleus in the Hoyle state (7.655 MeV) were more than 7.716 MeV or less than 7.596 MeV, our Universe would have almost no carbon. Because this range is so narrow, Hoyle concluded, "A common sense interpretation of the facts suggests that a super intellect has monkeyed with physics, as well as with chemistry and biology, and that there are no blind forces worth speaking about in nature. The numbers one calculates from the facts seem to me so overwhelming as to put this conclusion almost beyond question."[21]

Perhaps you disagree with Hoyle, but consider now the four fundamental forces: gravity, which you are probably familiar with; the electromagnetic force, which we see with magnets; the strong nuclear force, which holds together protons in the core of an atom; and the

---

18. Roger Penrose, YouTube, October 2, 2009, https://www.youtube.com/watch?v=WhGdVMBk6Zo (accessed January 24, 2025).

19. "Universe 101," NASA, February 21, 2024, https://wmap.gsfc.nasa.gov/universe/bb_cosmo_infl.html (accessed January 23, 2025).

20. T. Otsuka, et al., "α-Clustering in Atomic Nuclei from First Principles with Statistical Learning and the Hoyle State Character," *Nature Communications*, April 27, 2022, https://www.nature.com/articles/s41467-022-29582-0 (accessed January 23, 2025).

21. Fred Hoyle, "The Universe: Past and Present Reflections," *Engineering and Science*, vol. 45, issue 2 (November 1981): 8–12.

weak nuclear force, which is responsible for radioactive decay. The strengths of all these forces were set within the first fraction of a second after Creation. The strong nuclear force within atoms is 10^{36} times stronger than gravity. Without the strong nuclear force, which holds protons and neutrons together, there would only be hydrogen and none of the other elements that are required for complex life. Without the electromagnetic force, complex chemistry wouldn't exist, which is also required for complex life, nor would there be light. If any one of these values were altered, then the Universe could not exist. The numbers relating to the probabilities that the fundamental forces exist by chance are also mind-numbing, so I will just give one more example: "if the ratio between the strong nuclear force and the electromagnetic force had been off by the tiniest fraction of the tiniest fraction—by even one part in 100,000,000,000,000,000— then no stars could have ever formed at all."[22] Geraint F. Lewis and Luke A. Barnes summarized the dynamic perfectly: "An individual atom is unimaginably small, and its protons, neutrons and electrons smaller still. Their properties might seem like mere textbook technicalities, and yet their role in how the Universe plays out is enormous. The smallest ingredients of the Universe dramatically affect its bigger structures, especially the chemistry of life. It really is the case of the elemental tail wagging the cosmic dog."[23]

This brings us to gravity, without which there would be no coalescing of matter, and there wouldn't be any planets, stars, or complex organisms. Maybe you will take Sheldon Lee Cooper's word for it: "If gravity were slightly more powerful, the Universe would collapse into a

---

22. Eric Metaxas, "Science Increasingly Makes the Case for God," *Wall Street Journal* (December 25, 2014).

23. Geraint F. Lewis and Luke A. Barnes, *A Fortunate Universe: Life in a Finely Tuned Cosmos* (Cambridge University Press, November 2016).

ball. Also, if gravity were slightly less powerful, the Universe would fly apart and there'd be no stars or planets. It's just that gravity is precisely as strong as it needs to be. And if the ratio of the electromagnetic force to the strong force wasn't 1 percent, life wouldn't exist. What are the odds that would happen all by itself?"[24] Young Sheldon gets the science right, but Sir Isaac Newton connected the dots when he said, "Gravity explains the motion of the planets, but it cannot explain *who* sets the planets in motion." Gravity does not have a cause; there is no pushing or pulling mechanism that can be explained by materialistic means.

But it's not just gravity that should give the secularist angina. There are over a dozen laws of physics that must exist precisely as they are in order for us to exist. If the Universe were randomly created, there would be no expectations for laws. Where do these laws of physics come from? They aren't created by scientists; they are discovered by scientists. These laws exist independently of us and the Universe. They are not subject to time; they are the same today as they were yesterday and will be the same tomorrow. While they exist as concepts, they have real-world effects that must be obeyed. If there are laws that must be obeyed, then it logically follows that Someone created these laws, because laws require a Lawmaker. This Lawmaker must be someone who predates the Universe and exists outside of the Universe (Colossians 1:17). Secularists say that belief in God is incompatible with science, but it is the secularists who are incompatible with the Lawmaker.

Now you also need to consider that intertwined with the laws of physics are the fundamental constants. There are more than twenty-five fundamental physical constants of nature that determine how the Universe is structured. Between every physical quantity (e.g., mass and

---

24. Jaffar Mahmood, "A Crisis of Faith and Octopus Aliens," *Young Sheldon*, season 2, episode 3, Warner Bros., 2018.

time, length and mass, energy and time, and so on) there is a physical constant that ties them together.[25] The values of the constants could literally be anything, but they were set during Creation. If the ratios of *any* of these constants were slightly different, then the Universe would not exist, nor would we. Looking at the relative strengths of the four fundamental forces with gravity as the reference point (32 feet/second squared), the weak nuclear force is 10^{34} times gravity, the electromagnetic force is 10^{37} times greater than gravity, and the weak nuclear force is 10^{40} times greater than gravity. Those are a lot of zeros, so if the strength of gravity was increased or decreased by even an infinitesimal amount, then the life-supporting world as we know it could not exist. Consider next the fine structure constant, which governs the strength of the electromagnetic force. It is known as α (alpha) and is equal to $\sim 1/137$. If α deviated by as little as 4 percent, once again no carbon would exist, nor would life[26]. Now consider the cosmological constant, known as Λ (lambda). The cosmological constant, not to be confused with Hubble's "constant," represents the energy density of a force that opposes gravity. It is a highly fine-tuned and very small number (2.888×10^{-122} or a decimal followed by 120 zeroes then 2888[27]). If this constant differed slightly, the Universe would collapse upon itself or end up empty.

Perhaps some people don't appreciate the beauty of the design of the Universe because it can't be seen. These forces and constants are part of the "invisible" things that are referenced in the Creed. It's a lot

25. Starts with a Bang, "Ask Ethan: How Many Constants Define Our Universe?" Big Think, August 18, 2023, https://bigthink.com/starts-with-a-bang/how-many-constants-universe/ (accessed January 24, 2025).

26. Richard Feynman, *QED: The Strange Theory of Light and Matter*.

27. John D. Barrow, Douglas J. Shaw, "The Value of the Cosmological Constant," *General Relativity and Gravitation* 43 (May 16, 2011), https://arxiv.org/abs/1105.3105 (accessed January 24, 2025).

easier to picture a finely crafted watch with multiple gears. If one of those gears is not the right size, the watch doesn't work. Physical laws and constants alone can't create life, but they allow for the necessary environment and conditions. An erratic universe would make it very difficult for life to survive and flourish. Secularists propose that alternate universes may have laws of physics and constants that are different from our own, but there is no proof for any of this, and it still doesn't answer who fine-tuned ours. It certainly wasn't a blind watchmaker.

CHEMISTRY

Immediately after the Big Bang, there would not have been any chemistry, as the only elements in the Universe were hydrogen and helium. The fusion occurring within stars would go on to produce ninety additional elements, which allow for complex chemistry. Sixty elements can be found in the human body, and approximately thirty play key roles within the body. Believers in evolutionary theory tend to focus on biological evolution (which I discuss below); however, what is commonly disregarded, and intentionally so, is that before you can even discuss biological evolution one has to solve for chemical evolution: How did the first living cell arise from simple nonliving chemicals in an undirected chemical process? Why don't more people understand this gating problem with evolutionary theory? Once again, a picture is worth a thousand lies. No doubt you have seen some version of an origin of life illustration showing lighting hitting a murky pond with some phosphorus,[28] and *bada bing*, it's alive, it's alive, it's alive, and it's pronounced *Frankensteen*! Those illustrations

---

28. Nell Greenfieldboyce, "How a Building Block of Life Got Created in a Flash," NPR, March 16, 2021, https://www.npr.org/2021/03/16/977769884/how-a-building-block-of-life-got-created-in-a-flash (accessed January 24, 2025).

are laughable because it is commonly accepted that only living organisms can achieve both homeostasis and reproduction, and Louis Pasteur's observation that "Life can only come from life" has never been refuted. Pasteur also proved that rotten meat does not create flies and that spontaneous generation is not a thing. When secularists advocate for the primordial soup theory, they sound an awful lot like seventeenth-century chemist Jan Baptiste van Helmont, who thought he created mice using dirty shirts and wheat.

Even if you were able to get a single living cell from the Flying Spaghetti Monster taking an electrifying dump in a pond to create a primordial soup, how does that cell replicate? Without a replication function, there wouldn't be any new cells, and once the cell dies, the life form is terminated. If this magical cell did magically start to replicate, then there would just be more of the same original cell. There are not going to be any new functions or features, unless you are counting on some magical mutations. (In the biology section I discuss mutations and provide more insight into the importance of the information found in cells.) Moreover, when a cell divides, it needs to pass on specific information. But there is no accounting for the spontaneous arrival, storage, and transmission of information in these origin-of-life fairy tales. For now, take a minute and think about how ludicrous abiogenesis (the development of a living organism from nonliving matter) truly is, and while you are thinking about it, think about the fact that you *can* think about it. Not only can you think about it, but so can I and everyone we know. But I'll discuss consciousness in Part III.

What is life? It's not a soup of chemicals. Life requires functioning cells. *Functioning* is the operative word. Even the simplest cell is highly complex. The more scientists learn about the complexity of the cell, the further and further away they are from being able to

fully understand it, let alone replicate it. There are an infinite number of ways for a cell not to form. Chemical evolution has no logical
or practical starting point. Dr. James Tour issued a challenge to other
scientists, calling on them to prove *any* of the five fundamental problems he sees for abiogenesis).[29] The five fundamental problems are the
linking of amino acids into chains (i.e., polypeptides), the linking of
nucleotides into RNA molecules, the linking of simple sugars (i.e.,
monosaccharides) into chains known as polysaccharides, the origin of
biological information, and the assembly of components into a cell.

No one has taken him up on the challenge. And that challenge
is to merely create a simple cell. For more complex organisms, the
problem of their origin is exponentially more difficult. All of life is
made of proteins, and in order to have proteins, you need amino
acids, which are the building blocks of proteins. There are twenty
different amino acids that are used to make proteins. You also need
sugars (e.g., ribose) as well as nucleic acids for DNA and RNA. You
need lipids (i.e., fats) to make complicated cell walls that are semi-
permeable, which is no easy task. Trying to get life out of some
random lightning-infused concoction is highly improbable because
the ingredients that are necessary for some parts of a cell preclude
the making of other things necessary for the cell. The conditions to
make amino acids are the wrong conditions to make sugars. While
nitrogen fosters amino acids, it prevents sugars from forming. Life
chemistry requires homochirality[30]—the same way your right hand

---

29. Dr. James Tour, "Can Scientists Answer These Questions? RNA, Abiogenesis, Chemical Natural Selection & More," YouTube, August 24, 2023, https://www.youtube.com/
watch?v=MmykRoelTzU (accessed January 24, 2025).

30. Danielle Sedbrook, "Must the Molecules of Life Always Be Left-Handed or Right-Handed?"
Smithsonian Magazine, July 28, 2016, https://www.smithsonianmag.com/space/must-all-mol-
ecules-life-be-left-handed-or-right-handed-180959956/ (accessed January 24, 2025).

needs a right-handed glove and your left hand needs a left-handed glove. Since sugars are only right-handed and amino acids are only left-handed, there's just no way this occurred randomly.

Unfortunately for the secularist, time is never going to come to the rescue when trying to solve the abiogenesis puzzle with prebiotic soup because organic molecules decompose rapidly, and these molecules trend toward disorder and decomposition, not life. Every now and again, you will see some pronouncement in which the secularists claim they have made some new discovery toward creating life from chemicals, but rest assured, they have cheated. The cheating usually comes in the form of using premade molecules in fabricated environments. What you will never read in these stories is that the scientists had an outcome that they were trying to achieve and then reverse engineered some chemicals and environments to achieve this desired outcome. Rarely does anyone ever stop and ask: If you are reverse engineering something, aren't you admitting that the end product was engineered? Materialists are uncomfortable asking that question, because the follow-up question is: Who is the engineer?

BIOLOGY

"The beauty of a living thing is not the atoms that go into it, but the way those atoms are put together. Information distilled over 4 billion years of biological evolution." That is a perfect example of a secularist's platitude. Once you scratch beneath the surface of that statement, you understand why it is hollow. First, for information to be distilled, you must start with information. In the same way that laws require a lawmaker, information requires an author. Second, once again, everything in the Universe trends toward disorder and chaos. However, the invisible force that is entropy can be reversed, or at least held at bay, by an intelligent Agent who produces information resulting in order.

I have already discussed why the picture of lightning striking a bunch of kak in a mud puddle to create life is farcical; however, Rudolph Zallinger's "March of Progress" illustration for the *Early Man* volume of *Life Nature Library* is the ultimate secularist piece of propaganda. This drawing of the gapless evolution of man from monkey is singularly responsible for ingraining the tall tale of evolution into "settled science." In the minds of the secularists, there's no quantum leap of logic required to believe that if that single cell formed in the turd puddle, then given enough time, a monkey is going to turn into a human. To assuage their critics there have been many riffs[31, 32] on this fairy tale showing how the gaps were filled along the way in a perfect time-lapsed sequence of species akin to building a house from the foundation up. Yet it's notable that the riffs usually skip the part where somehow along the magical evolutionary trail a particular organism decided it wanted to fly and developed all the necessary functions for that apparently insignificant feat. Darwin may have given atheists reason to be intellectually fulfilled, but unfortunately, not reason to be intellectually honest.

Now, before anyone throws the book down, please know that I am not denying *natural selection*. But natural selection is not the same thing as evolution. Botanist Arthur Harris noted, "Natural selection may explain the survival of the fittest but cannot explain the arrival of the fittest."[33] Of course, there are gradual changes to organisms via

---

31. Mark Belan, "The 4 Billion Year Path of Human Evolution," Visual Capitalist, June 9, 2023, https://www.visualcapitalist.com/path-of-human-evolution/ (accessed January 24, 2025).

32. Carl Sagan, "COSMOS—Evolution," YouTube, February 11, 2009, https://www.youtube.com/watch?v=gZpsVSVRsZk (accessed January 24, 2025).

33. Arthur Harris, review of Hugo de Vries, *Species and Varieties: Their Origin by Mutation: Lectures Delivered at the University of California* (United States: Open Court Publishing Company, 1904).

random variation and natural selection, but this does not result in creating new functionality or a creating a new type of organism. This is preprogrammed adaptation with the fittest surviving, rather than the creation of a new species. New functionality requires a design plan that contains information. Unguided processes end in chaos because there is no mechanism to envision an end product. Interim stages of a randomly evolving system are useless when there is no endgame. Michael Behe is credited with coming up with the phrase "irreducibly complex" to describe a single system that has component parts where if any of those parts are not present, or are nonfunctional, then the entire system doesn't work. He uses a five-part mousetrap as an example. Without any of the individual parts, such as the spring or the catch, the mousetrap doesn't work. In fact, without any of the five parts, it is not a mouse trap. An unguided process could never end up creating distinct component parts that are only useful unless they were used in conjunction and in furtherance of an unrelated function.

It would be absurd for someone to think that today's jet airplanes have evolved via an unguided process from what Orville and Wilbur launched at Kitty Hawk in 1903, although a Darwinist might claim the helicopter to be some sort of mutant intermediate species. Our bodies are exponentially more complex and well beyond the design or manufacturing capabilities used to make today's planes, yet the secularists continue to claim that we humans have evolved from some simple life form. Within our bodies there are a multitude of irreducibly complex systems. There are bio-machines on the molecular level without which we would not be alive. There are many examples. Consider our auditory system, which is made up of the auricle, auditory canal, tympanic membrane, malleus, incus, stapes, oval window, manubrium, and so on. The secularists tell us that all of these parts randomly evolved without any plan in order that an organism could hear. Did you ever consider asking how this first organism knew that there was something to hear and then achieved that goal of hearing? Now extrapolate that out to the other senses. There's no explanation as to how or why these functions would *initiate*. I would like to be able to fly—please let me know if you know anyone who can help me come up with a plan to evolve into a flying man.

People can certainly be guilty of apophenia (finding patterns in unrelated events or items) or being fooled by randomness,[34] but secularists, particularly in the science community, subvert laypeople's common sense by gaslighting them with claims of randomness and chance. It seems logical that snow falls and accumulates randomly. However, when discussing randomness, it is critical to understand that it is a *preliminary* determination. Order and complexity nullify randomness, and sometimes that snow accumulation may not be so random.[35] When you recognize order and design, you can't unsee it any more than you can unsee who Kaiser Söze really is. Once randomness is eliminated as an answer, it's only logical to then search for a Creator.

Life must be designed from the top down, otherwise you must believe that the human body randomly came together like a Rube-Goldberg machine. Not unlike a plane, or other complex machines, the human body is a wonderfully designed machine made up of many critical subsystems (integumentary system, muscular system, skeletal system, nervous system, endocrine system, circulatory system, lymphatic system, respiratory system, digestive system, urinary system, reproductive system, and so on), all of which are integrated to work together within the

---

34. Nassim Nicholas Taleb, *Fooled by Randomness* (New York: Random House, 2005).

35. Melanie Renzulli, "These Amazing Italian Gardens Are Shaped like a Violin," Italofile, February 15, 2021, https://www.italofile.com/vanvitelli-violin-caserta/ (accessed January 24, 2025).

overall functional design of the master machine. All it takes is for you to admit that if just one part is designed, then we know there is a Creator.

It's difficult to actually quantify how many subsystems or body parts there are, if you consider everything from an organ, like the heart, to molecular-level ribosomes, which are responsible for protein synthesis. Think about your heart as a machine that is integrated into your circulatory, respiratory, and nervous systems. It beats more than 100,000 times a day while pumping 2,000 gallons of fluid that transports necessary nutrients while removing waste products all through 60,000 miles of plumbing (your veins, arteries, and capillaries). That's quite a machine. The scoffer will tell you that I have a common ancestor with a whale. The blue whale is the largest living animal we know of today. They weigh 40,000 pounds and their hearts weigh over 400 pounds, which is about 640 times the size of a human heart. Instead of looking at artists' representations of what evolution supposedly looks like, take a look at the real world around you. Think of the unimaginable amount of faith in randomness and chance it takes to look at the picture of a blue whale's heart[36] and believe that it was randomly formed and then randomly shrunk to fit a human.

The heart is only *one* such machine that is highly integrated into the master machine (that is, you) without which you wouldn't function. The obviousness of design is why we are surprised when we see someone like Jean Libbera, a.k.a. the "Double-Bodied Man." He was called a freak because he had two arms, two legs, and a partially formed head protruding out of his chest. However, that sort of haphazardness is what we would expect if body parts were randomly

36. Mai Nguyen, "How Scientists Preserved a 440-Pound Blue Whale Heart," *WIRED*, July 2, 2017, https://www.wired.com/story/how-scientists-preserved-a-440-pound-blue-whale-heart/ (accessed January 28, 2025).

generated. Newton made the same observation when he asked the following with Proverbs 9:10 in mind:

> Can it be by accident that all birds beasts & men have their right side & left side alike shaped (except in their bowells) & just two eyes & no more on either side the face & just two ears on either side the head & a nose with two holes & no more between the eyes & one mouth under the nose & either two fore legs or two wings or two arms on the sholders & two legs on the hipps one on either side & no more? Whence arises this uniformity in all their outward shapes but from the counsel & contrivance of an Author? Whence is it that the eyes of all sorts of living creatures are transparent to the very bottom & the only transparent members in the body, having on the outside an hard transparent skin, & within transparent juyces with a crystalline Lens in the middle & a pupil before the Lens all of them so truly shaped & fitted for vision, that no Artist can mend them? Did blind chance know that there was light & what was its refraction & fit the eys of all creatures after the most curious manner to make use of it? These & such like considerations always have & ever will prevail with man kind to beleive that there is a being who made all things & has all things in his power & who is therfore to be feared."[37]

The human body is a beautiful thing to behold, yet oddly, "bad design" or "stupid design" are common arguments made by scoffers.

---

37. Isaac Newton, *A Short Schem of the True Religion*. Original spelling preserved.

The thinking goes something along the lines that an all-knowing God would not create life that could only exist inside of an apparently infinitesimal and obscure terrarium. Furthermore, why would an omniscient God create beings who get sick and get hurt, and whose bodies inevitably fail them? As far as the first point goes, the opposite view seems more logical, because if one thinks about the care and precision that went into making Earth specifically for us somewhere in an otherwise hostile Universe, that, to me, shows a lot of care. Regarding the second point, death only entered the world because of sin (Romans 5:12), and sin is an unfortunate byproduct of free will. While you may not like that answer, it's His creation, and it's pretty hard to argue with omniscience.

The "stupid design" argument is stupid. It's stupid for lots of objective reasons. For instance, scoffers mock the design of the human mouth because it allows for the possibility of choking. However, one of the signatures of elegance in design engineering is concurrent design. Thus, it is an elegant design where one hole can be used to eat, breathe, and speak. He could have given the blowhards a blowhole like He did with dolphins, but He chose not to. For those scoffers so worried about choking and unable to use a little common sense or good manners by not talking with their mouths full, God sent Henry Heimlich.

The bad design argument extends to all sorts of body parts such as the appendix, tonsils, coccyx (tail bone), vertebrate eye, laryngeal nerve, panda's thumb, pelvic bone in whales, and so on. Yet as scientific discovery advances, the bad design argument consistently gets refuted, usually without atonement, shame, or consequence. Junk DNA was thought to be evidence of evolution because there would be no reason to design junk. It turns out that as scientists learn more, they have realized that DNA that was labeled as junk is not junk after all. It's just more complex than could be previously understood. It's the secularists' lack of humility that prevents them from admitting that they don't understand a function; therefore, out of ignorance, they conclude it is functionless and therefore junk.

It's important to note that while it's one thing to make the bad design argument a philosophical matter, it can become much more serious when it is used in a medical context. It seems harmless when scientists try to enhance hand functionality using a robotic prosthetic to create a "third thumb,"[38] although one must wonder, if this was such a great improvement, why it didn't happen through selective adaptations. The concerns arise with dysteleologists, who assume the absence of purpose in life and nature. Their worldview can lead to horrific outcomes for patients. We now have doctors who might give Mengele pause. They prescribe cross-sex hormones and try to turn women into men and men into women by castrating boys and inverting their penises to form what they call neovaginas. Moreover, there are now millions of patients who may end up suffering from depression for the rest of their lives because they will be taking weight loss drugs that paralyze their stomachs. It turns out that the gut is responsible for more than 90 percent of serotonin production.[39] Moreover, these drugs have negative effects on other organs.[40] Messing with one of the body's systems can have serious consequences on another. This is the problem with life scientists, who "know better" than to

---

38. Craig Brierley, "Getting to Grips with an Extra Thumb," University of Cambridge, May 29, 2024, https://www.cam.ac.uk/stories/third-thumb (accessed January 28, 2025).

39. Senthil Vel Rajan Rajaram Manoharan and Rohit Madan, "GLP-1 Agonists Can Affect Mood: A case of Worsened Depression on Ozempic," *Innovations in Clinical Neuroscience*, June 2024, https://pmc.ncbi.nlm.nih.gov/articles/PMC11208009/ (accessed January 28, 2025

40. Yan Xie, Taeyoung Choi, and Ziyad Al-Aly, "Mapping the effectiveness and risks of GLP-1 receptor agonists," *Nature*, January 20, 2025, https://www.nature.com/articles/s41591-024-03412-w (accessed January 28, 2025)

consider all of the implications of integrated engineering within the intricately designed and selectively adapted human body. On other fronts, the unintended consequences of creating mirror organisms[41] and gene editing will inevitably cause a lot of problems as well. There's little to no outrage when scientists admit that "We don't know what we don't know with gene editing."[42] The point is not to obstruct or delay research; the point is to make sure it is conducted wisely and ethically. The mantra of "move fast and break things" is not acceptable when lives and souls are at stake. The real and present danger caused by the secularist scientists who are unwilling to consider facts that are contrary to their worldview brings to mind the quote from the *Chernobyl* character Valery Legasov: "Every lie we tell incurs a debt to the truth. Sooner or later, that debt is paid."[43]

❁ ❁ ❁

It's easy for people to acknowledge that airplanes are created, because they can go to a Boeing plant and see them being built. Life is different, because we don't see someone building it. This leads to the next reason we know life is the result of a Creator. Life as we know it is possible because information drives the process, and information requires an intelligent source. Dr. Werner Gitt noted that "All technological systems as well as all constructed objects, from pins to works of art, have been produced by means of information. None of

41. Simon Makin, "Creating 'Mirror Life' Could Be Disastrous, Scientists Warn," Scientific American, December 14, 2024, https://www.scientificamerican.com/article/creating-mirror-life-could-be-disastrous-scientists-warn/ (accessed January 28, 2025).

42. Betsy McKay, "Doctors Can Now Edit the Genes Inside Your Body," *Wall Street Journal*, March 11, 2024, https://www.wsj.com/health/pharma/doctors-can-now-edit-the-genes-inside-your-body-4c8e1aea (accessed January 28, 2025).

43. Johan Renck, "Vichnaya Pamyat," *Chernobyl*, season 1, episode 5, HBO, 2019.

these artifacts came into existence through some form of self-organization of matter, but all of them were preceded by establishing the required information."[44]

All cells are highly sophisticated. There is a lot more going on than mere chemical reactions (such as metabolism), and none of this is random. Within cells there is the storage, transfer, and processing of information. Molecular processing consists of not just replicating DNA but also the additional processing of information. The discovery of DNA enabled us to begin to understand that information is as fundamental to the Universe as matter and energy. The DNA in your body could be stretched back and forth from the Earth to Pluto (~10 billion miles). What incredible engineering it takes not only to make it all fit inside our cells but also for it to make sense. The double helix structure of DNA enables the information to make sense because genetic information is stored in code form. DNA polymerase replicates DNA, RNA polymerase synthesizes RNA from DNA, and ribosomes use RNA to build proteins. These four molecules are essential to all life on earth. Proteins drive life by providing shape and structure for cells and are responsible for a wide range of roles, including in the functions of muscles, nerves, and enzymes. Proteins are molecules made up of a chain in amino acids, similar to words in a sentence. Creating a protein (sentence) from scratch requires a gene that contains the requisite information, as genes author the protein "sentences" amino acid by amino acid, or "word" by "word." Each gene is a segment of DNA containing a series of pairs of nucleotides: adenine (A), cytosine (C), guanine (G), and thymine (T).

There are twenty amino acids that form proteins. The shortest proteins (sentences) are made up of 100–150 amino acids (words).

---

44. Werner Gitt, *In the Beginning Was Information* (Green Forest, AR: Master Books, 2006), 53.

The amino acids (words) have to be in the right place for the protein (sentence) to be functional. Thus, at each site on the protein (the slot for the word in the sentence), there is a 1 in 20 chance that the correct amino acid (word) will appear. Now, factoring in the second site, there is a 1 in 400 chance that the two correct amino acids (words) appear. For a chain of amino acids that is ten sites long, there would be 10,000,000,000,000 possible combinations. The shortest proteins contain 100–150 amino acids, so for a protein with 150 amino acids, there are 1×10^{195} possibilities. Now factor in that amino acids are joined by peptide bonds, and there is a 1 out of 2 chance of getting the right peptide. I am going to stop because the permutations become ridiculous. If you believe the universe to be about 14 billion years old, that is 4×10^{17} seconds, and there are roughly 10^{80} elementary particles (protons, neutrons, and electrons) in the whole Universe, then there is just not enough time or opportunities to randomly create even one simple protein. The complexity is further compounded because of protein folding, which I won't go into the details about here. I doubt even Lloyd Christmas would like the chances, but if you want the full Monty on the complexity and the math, check out Doug Axe's book *Undeniable*.

Very few amino acid sequences can form functional proteins because there is nothing about the sequence in our genetic code that would dictate meaning. That information must pre-exist, and it must be authored by an intelligent being. This is usually about the time when a scoffer mentions the Infinite Monkey Theorem, which says that if you put enough monkeys at typewriters, eventually one of them will produce Shakespeare. But once you realize that most of the monkeys are going to spend more time defecating on the typewriters than pressing the keys, you can look at the math. The odds of randomly typing one line from Shakespeare's sonnet, "Shall I compare thee to a summer's day?" are 10^{690}—and remember that by their own current reckoning, the Universe is 13.8 billion years old and is not infinite.[45] One scoffer has a theory that cumulative selections function as a probability amplifier, thereby making the improbable probable, if not certain, because multiple things going on at the same time reduce the probability. He developed Weasel Ware,[46] which he claims can produce more information from the software than what was put in and thus provides a model for randomly generating usable information. But this sleight of hand is characteristically weaselly and ends as a Shakespearean tragedy, once you realize that the program is written to target a specific predetermined sentence. There is nothing random about working toward a known result. Try this experiment instead: blindfold a scoffer, hand them a mixed-up Rubik's Cube, and tell them to solve it. They will probably admit they can't. Now take the blindfold off and give them access to YouTube. They may then come back to you with the cube "solved." But then ask the question: "Who said that was the answer I was looking for?" They had knowledge of an end point and moved toward that end point. Undirected natural selection has no such end point it is seeking. And remember, just one functioning protein is many more times complex and has many times more possible permutations than a Rubik's Cube.

It's obvious that the evidence of design in our genome relegates evolution theory to the dustbin and that mutations are another false god of the secularists. In general, mutations are a net bad for us because there are an infinite number of ways changes through mutations can

---

45. Patrick McIntyre, "Monkeys with Typewriters Theorem," YouTube, December 15, 2008, https://www.youtube.com/watch?v=pDUn7dDigvI (accessed January 28, 2025).

46. "Weasel Ware—Evolutionary Simulation," Evolutionary Informatics, https://evoinfo.org/weasel (accessed January 28, 2025).

harm us and a limited number of ways they can be beneficial. Of course, mutations can result in small-scale variations by modifying existing forms or functions used in specific environments. The mutation that enabled the "fittest" to survive will most likely have a deleterious effect on the organism's ability to survive other environments because complex organisms suffer a high cost of selection.[47] Once again, the math provides additional support that shows we aren't the result of mutant monkeys. No one can say with certainty where, when, and how the "modern" human arose, but Haldane's Dilemma states that in ten million years the human population could generate no more than 1,666 beneficial mutations. This means that there's just not enough time to randomly monkey around with the three billion base pairs in the genome to get enough beneficial changes when there will be a whole lot more harmful mutations. Motoo Kimura's Neutral Theory attempted to refute Haldane's Dilemma; however, his theory was effectively rejected by Andrew Kern and Matthew Hahn.[48]

Let's consider natural selection using an example we are all familiar with. I'll use dogs, since almost everyone can relate to man's best friend. There are over four hundred breeds of dogs, but they are all ultimately related to the big grey wolf. Because they are all from the same species, the genetic variability of what can be bred amongst Labradoodles, Goldendoodles, or any other breed is limited to God's design and preprogrammed adaptations for dogs. There are not infinite possibilities; in fact, there are only three general types of skulls for dogs: dolichocephalic (large nasal cavity for hunting and sniffing),

47. Ronald Fisher, *The Genetical Theory of Natural Selection* (Garden City, NY: Dover Publications, 1958).

48. Andrew D. Kern, Matthew W. Hahn, "The Neutral Theory in Light of Natural Selection," *Molecular Biology and Evolution*, vol. 35, issue 6 (June 2018): 1366–71, https://academic.oup.com/mbe/article/35/6/1366/4990884?login=false (accessed January 28, 2025).

mesocephalic (equal proportions of the cranium and nasal cavities), and brachycephalic (large cranium, small snout).[49] You can breed them to make them cuter, but you can't breed wings into dogs and make them fly.

Now let's take a look in the mirror. Paleoanthropologists and geneticists now universally agree that *Homo sapiens* and Neanderthals interbred.[50] Despite what you have been told, there are not different species of humans. If they were able to interbreed, that means that they must be members of the same species but maybe had differently shaped skulls. This should not be a surprise, because strange stuff happens when a lot of inbreeding occurs. Around 1550, the House of Habsburgs thought it would be a good idea to stop introducing new genes into their family tree, and this went on for about two hundred years. As a result, people in this family ended up with the Habsburg jaw (Google it for a visual). This type of behavior would be consistent with other physical distinguishments, such as the Cro-Magnon forehead and epicanthic folds on eyelids. Adaptation of the PDE10A gene amongst the Bajau people of Malaysia and the Philippines results in a spleen that provides them with a larger reservoir of oxygenated red blood cells. These are examples of natural selection in action that results in the promotion of a particular trait within the species, not the creation of a new species. This is an adaptation of an existing function, not the formation of a new function; however, it wouldn't surprise me to see cocksures cite the Bajau as a transitional species to Mariner from *Waterworld*. There is incredible

49. Adrienne Farricelli, The Three Types of Dog Heads (Skulls), September 29, 2000, https://dogdiscoveries.com/curiosity/the-three-different-types-of-dog-heads-skulls (accessed March 23, 2025).

50. Princeton University, " 'A History of Contact': Geneticists Are Rewriting the Narrative of Neanderthals and Other Ancient Humans," Phys.org, July 11, 2024, https://phys.org/news/2024-07-history-contact-geneticists-rewriting-narrative.html (accessed January 28, 2025).

diversity in appearance amongst *Homo sapiens*, which you would see if you put Sultan Kösen (the world's tallest man at 8'3"), Chandra Bahadur Dangi (the world's shortest man at 1'9.5"), Nikolai Valuev (Russian boxer with a protruding forehead), Justin Bieber (a Canadian), and Kisenosato Yutaka (a sumo wrestler) all in the same room. But if their bodies were dug up after being in the ground for some unknown amount of time, you can bet a different story would be told by the secularists and that they would likely all be categorized as different species. In contrast, Jesus' genealogy provides a straight line from Adam to Jesus, so we know the history of man. While the "settled science" relating to the divergence between Neanderthals and *Homo sapiens* is constantly evolving,[51] the truth is not.

I know, I know; you were also told your DNA is so close to simians that you must be related. Not so. A recent study[52] revealed that DNA sequencing of a human Y chromosome was 26.2 percent similar to a chimpanzee, 25.1 percent similar to a gorilla, and 23.1 percent similar to a Bornean orangutan. The chimpanzee was 19.8 percent similar to the gorilla and 30.8 percent similar to the Bornean orangutan. The minimal similarities of Y chromosomes, which are only found in males, undermines the theory of evolution because they should be most similar, since there is no recombination with a homologous chromosome (the alignment of paired chromosomes from a male and female parent). This again is no surprise because these animals have

51. Dorothea Mylopotamitaki, et al., "Homo sapiens Reached the Higher Latitudes of Europe by 45,000 Years Ago," *Nature* 626 (January 31, 2024): 341–46, https://www.nature.com/articles/s41586-023-06923-7?utm_medium=affiliate&utm_source=commission_junction&utm_campaign=CONR_PF018_ECOM_GL_PHSS_ALWYS_DEEPLINK&utm_content=textlink&utm_term=PID100024933&CJEVENT=0a3fb72de6f311ee81a00a250a82b82a (accessed January 28, 2025).

52. Kateryna D. Makova, et al., "The Complete Sequence and Comparative Analysis of Ape Sex Chromosomes," *Nature* 630 (May 29, 2024): 401–411, https://www.nature.com/articles/s41586-024-07473-2 (accessed January 28, 2025).

their own unique features and generally cannot interbreed. From a design perspective, it makes perfect sense why there are some similarities in the genetic code of various creatures. The software engineers at Microsoft first designed Word and then created the rest of the Office product suite. Some of that code from Word was reused for Excel and PowerPoint, but the filename extensions .doc, .xls, and .ppt delineate them and prevent them from being combined. There's no reason to think the Ultimate Engineer wouldn't do the same.

* * *

If life evolved, how and why did replication come about? Earlier I discussed the concept of systems being irreducibly complex. Now pan out and consider how humans are irreducibly complex. How would sexual reproduction come to be when two distinct and incredibly complex parties with fully functioning reproductive organs are needed from the start? Especially if there was no Barry White. Males could go blind trying to self-replicate, so what could have been the precursor for their sexual reproduction? The Ultimate Engineer tells us that there is no chicken or egg problem. The anatomical structures of men and women were created perfectly complementary for two to become one flesh (Mark 10:8). Each party's gamete contributes 1.5 billion letters of DNA to a new, unique, three-billion-letter genome code, and some 6,480 hours later, a child is born. This child of God is born and will end up with 30 trillion cells, 200 types of tissue, hundreds of organs, and yards of blood vessels, all interacting together. Look at the SciePro complete model of the human body,[53] and it is absurd to think that all of those functioning parts came together randomly.

---

53. "Complete Human Anatomy," SciePro, https://www.sciepro.com/3d-models/complete-human-anatomy (accessed January 28, 2025).

Now that you understand that there is no reasonable chance that you are a monkey's uncle (or aunt) derived from randomly mutated proteins, think about how special you *really* are. Consider all of the things that had to happen for you to have been conceived (okay, maybe not *everything*). On average, a woman produces 300,000 to 400,000 eggs over her lifetime, and since a female is born with all her eggs, when your grandmother was carrying your mother, the egg that would be fertilized by your father was inside of your grandmother. As far as your father, a man will produce somewhere around a trillion sperm in his lifetime (1×10^{12}). I know it's awkward to think about, but you were conceived at the exact point in time when exactly one of those eggs and one of those sperm united. Lyrical Zen[54] provides some ancestral math to think about: In order to be born, you needed 2 parents, 4 grandparents, 8 great-grandparents, 16 second great-grandparents, 32 third great-grandparents, 64 fourth great-grandparents, 128 fifth great-grandparents, 256 sixth great-grandparents, 512 seventh great-grandparents, 1,024 eighth great-grandparents, 2,048 ninth great-grandparents, and 4,096 tenth great-grandparents. That's just going back ten generations. It's unfathomable to think of all the worldly events that happened so that you could be here today. God tells us that He knows scoffers believe that "all of us came into being by chance [and] when our lives are over, it will be just as if we had never been" (Wisdom 2:2 CEB). But for the rest of us, He has made it known that we are not the product of chance; rather, we are all part of His plan, because He knew us before we were formed in the womb (Jeremiah 1:5).

Panspermians would have us believe that life was planted on Earth

---

54. "Ancestral Mathematics," Lyrical Zen, August 12, 2019, https://lyricalzen.com/ancestral-mathematics/ (accessed January 28, 2025).

by aliens, but once again this requires some kind of a creator who is never identified. Secularists will also quote the anthropic principle, which states that we should not be surprised that all of these conditions exist since we are here to observe them. This isn't very helpful to their cause, since it conflates observing the conditions needed for life with a cause—telling me I am here to observe these wonders doesn't tell me who put me here. God told us He created the Universe and put us here.

GEOLOGY AND PALEONTOLOGY

Pangaea was the supercontinent that is believed to have existed prior to the current continents breaking apart into the recently accepted eight continents.[55] Matching footprints from dinosaurs found in Brazil and Cameroon[56] provide strong evidence that Pangaea existed. The timing of when and how quickly Pangaea separated into the current continents is hotly debated. The fact of the matter is that it's impossible to know what the Earth looked like before the Flood, and the Bible doesn't provide us with a lot of specificity. The Flood as a worldwide event caused by God is a common stumbling block for the faith. Despite Jesus having specifically affirmed its occurrence (Matthew 24:37), it just seems too unbelievable for many Christians. Since Jesus did affirm the Flood, our geological perspective of the Earth must be viewed in terms of the consequences of the Flood, and when you look carefully, the evidence is consistent with this perspective.

55. Nick Mortimer, et al., "Zealandia: Earth's Hidden Continent," *GSA Today*, vol. 27, issue 3 (March/April 2017): 27–35, https://rock.geosociety.org/gsatoday/archive/27/3/article/GSATG321A.1.htm (accessed January 28, 2025).

56. "Matching Dinosaur Footprints Found on Opposite Sides of the Atlantic Ocean," SMU News, August 23, 2024, https://www.smu.edu/news/research/matching-dinosaur-footprints-different-continents (accessed January 28, 2025).

The difficult questions that I always asked myself regarding the Flood were these: Where did all of that water come from, and where could it have all gone? It's certainly fantastical to think about the entire Earth underwater. However, if there were torrential rains everywhere for forty days and forty nights, you can begin to wrap your head around how much water that would be. Moreover, while that would have been a lot, an often-overlooked detail in the Flood account is that water also burst forth from within the Earth (Genesis 7:10–12). The Flood account also hints that the continental structure and surface of the Earth were significantly different before the Flood. It's universally accepted that the summit of Mount Everest was at one time the sea floor (there's a significant disagreement about how long ago that was the case), so if mountain ranges did not exist or were not as high, that would lessen the necessary depth to which the water had to rise in order to drown all air-breathing animals. I can visualize where the water came from and how it covered the Earth, but to me, the harder question was, Where did it all go? Regardless of the fact that presently more than 70 percent of the Earth is covered with water, it still seems like there is a post-Flood storage deficit. However, it's eye-opening to look at the math and a visualization relating the volume of the Earth compared to volume of the all the water on the Earth. Only 0.12 percent of the Earth's total volume is liquid water; thus, if every drop of water in the world was collected in a sphere, it would be just 869 miles across—about the size of Europe. As a side note, there's not a lot of air, either.[57] Moreover, 400 miles below the Earth's surface is a substance called *ringwoodite* that could hold more than three times the amount of water on the Earth's sur-

---

57. M. Özgür Nevres, "All the Earth's Water and Air," Our Planet, December 2, 2018, https://our-plnt.com/water-air-earth/ (accessed January 28, 2025).

face. So there's plenty of room within the Earth to hold all of the water from the Flood.

Once again, a misleading visualization has wrongly enabled the secularists to dominate the geological narrative and undermine God's story. We've all seen pictures of the clearly defined layers of the Grand Canyon known as the geological column. But how did those layers really get there? The "settled science" tells us that each of those layers was laid down over millennia and that the Colorado River carved through the layers over eons. Except that's not what happened, just like I am not related to a monkey. To understand what happened, think about the power of water when reading Noah's account. Floods and tsunamis regularly cause enormous destruction. Within my own lifetime, I have seen the damage caused by tsunamis in Indonesia (2004) and Japan (2011). In 1980, the eruption of Mount St. Helens caused wide-scale damage to the region and carved a sizeable canyon in just one day. In 2023, a 650-foot tsunami caused the Earth to shake for nine days.[58] In 2024, Hurricane Helene caused historic flooding. To our modern sensibilities, these were catastrophic events; however, they would be merely minor events in relation to the total destruction caused by Noah's Flood.

Once you look at recent destructive flooding events and use those inputs in a model that is applied to Noah's Flood, it makes it much easier to see how the Grand Canyon was more likely carved quickly and not over years. The films *Is Genesis History?* and *Mountains After the Flood*, written by Thomas Purifoy, Jr., do an outstanding job of having scientists explain the effects of Noah's Flood and debunk the

---

58. StudyFinds Staff, " 'Completely Baffled': 656-Foot Mega-Tsunami That Made the Earth Vibrate for 9 Days Stuns Scientists," StudyFinds, September 13, 2024, https://studyfinds.org/land-slide-earth-vibrate-9-days/ (accessed January 28, 2025).

idea that the strata we see in the Grand Canyon are the result of millennia of erosion as opposed to the rapid deposit of various layers of sediment. The secularists' view doesn't comport with what we see today when looking at flat rock layers in the Grand Canyon, which have smooth surfaces. The expectation would be that these surfaces would be rough and jagged after being exposed to the elements for millions of years. The secularists' view is also undermined by the massive folds in the rocks within the Grand Canyon, as these could only occur if the rocks were folded when they were soft during the Flood instead of the folds occurring when the rocks were hard and brittle, like they would be had they been there for millennia. Also, when looking at layers of strata, there is no evidence within the layers of long-term environmental effects—there are often no roots or burrowing organisms making their marks within the layers. Here's the Reverse Uno Card for believers: a polystrate fossil[59] is one that penetrates vertically through multiple geological layers and destroys the secularist narrative. Seeing a tree trunk penetrating "millions of years" of geological stratum ought to make you ask yourself if you are going to believe a secularist or your own eyes.

The geological record is just part of the problem for secularists. The other side of that coin is the fossil record. There is no plausible explanation for the appearance of the myriad of complex animals in the Cambrian period, all without transitional fossils. The global Flood account logically supports the fossil record as it exists. Although every layer contains saltwater creatures, marine animals were mostly buried in the first layers of sediment, which lines up with what the

---

59. Michael C. Rygel, "Ancient in situ lycopsid, probably Sigillaria, with attached stigmarian roots. Specimen is from the Joggins Formation (Pennsylvanian), Cumberland Basin, Nova Scotia," photograph, Wikipedia, https://en.wikipedia.org/wiki/Polystrate_fossil#/media/File:Lycopsid_joggins_mcr1.JPG (accessed January 30, 2025).

"settled science" calls the Paleozoic period. As the waters rose, land-living animals would have sought higher ground but were eventually buried later in the layers that correspond to the Mesozoic and Cenozoic periods. This layering process is also consistent with the fact that there is evidence of vertebrates' footprints in the lower layers yet most of the body parts are found in the higher layers. Recognizing that the sediment layers were rapidly laid down during the cataclysmic flooding allows you to answer how ocean-living stingrays got fossilized in Wyoming,[60] whales ended up buried in a desert in Peru,[61] and sharks ended up in Arkansas.[62] All the air-breathing animals that were not on Noah's ark were drowned and buried.

The secularists' view of the fossil record and history is replete with many contradictions that they can't explain. Well-preserved fossils undermine the "settled science" that the Earth is billions of years old. The fossil record shows bats and frogs that are very much the same today as their ancestors that are supposedly millions of years old. Even more curious are the many dinosaur fossils that still contain red blood cells, soft tissue, and even skin, which cannot survive millions of years.[63, 64] Whenever a "startling" new discovery is made,

60. "Stunning, 12.6" Fossil Stingray (Heliobatis)—Wyoming," Fossil Era, https://www.fossilera.com/fossils/stunning-12-6-fossil-stingray-heliobatis-wyoming (accessed January 28, 2025).

61. Will Dunham, "Ancient Whale from Peru Might Be Most Massive Animal Ever on Earth," Reuters, August 2, 2023, https://www.reuters.com/science/ancient-whale-peru-may-be-most-massive-animal-ever-earth-2023-08-02/ (accessed January 28, 2025).

62. Enrico de Lazaro, "Devonian Shark Fossil Found in Arkansas," Sci News, March 26, 2024, https://www.sci.news/paleontology/cosmoselachus-mehlingi-12796.html (accessed January 28, 2025).

63. Jeanne Timmons, "Researchers Look a Dinosaur in Its Remarkably Preserved Face," Ars Technica, January 25, 2023, https://arstechnica.com/science/2023/01/researchers-look-a-dinosaur-in-its-remarkably-preserved-face/?utm_medium=social&utm_social-type=owned&utm_source=twitter&utm_brand=ars (accessed January 28, 2025).

64. CBS News, "60 Minutes Presents: B-Rex," YouTube, December 26, 2010, https://www.youtube.com/watch?v=yJOQiyLFMNY (accessed January 28, 2025).

the secularists once again inevitably have to resort to monkeying with time in order to preserve their models and to save face.

Secularists are so confident in the "settled science" in large part because of their reliance on ^{14}C dating, but it turns out that this science is hardly settled. There many examples of problems with ^{14}C dating. Take, for instance, the testing done on the Vollosovitch mammoth. One part of the animal was dated 29,300 years old, while another part of the *same* animal was dated to be 44,000 years old. There are examples of freshly killed seals dated to be 1,300 years old.[65] In 2018, scientists found horse bones in Lehi, Utah, that they dated to the "last ice age" because the bones were buried in sediment that was dated to 16,000 years ago. A later study using radiocarbon dating showed the bones were no older than 340 years old.[66] A 2024 study stated that misunderstanding ancient diets resulted in having to change ^{14}C dating models for people in Central European Russia by some 900 years.[67] If the evidence doesn't fit the narrative, a new model is created.

One of the major problems with ^{14}C dating is that assumptions need to be made. Assumptions need to be made as to past conditions on Earth, and then extrapolations are made. Uniformitarians assume that the Earth is largely the same today as it has always been, thus enabling scientists to use ^{14}C levels as a measuring stick. Given the cataclysmic nature of the Flood, it seems likely that the Earth

65. Wakefield Dort, "The Mummified Seals of Southern Victoria Land, Antarctica," *Antarctic Research Series Terrestrial Biology* III (1978): 123–54.

66. Laura M. Holson, "An Ancient Horse Is Unearthed in a Utah Backyard," *The New York Times*, May 3, 2018, https://www.nytimes.com/2018/05/03/science/horse-skeleton-utah.html (accessed January 28, 2025).

67. Leibniz-Zentrum für Archäologie, "New Approach to Carbon-14 Dating Corrects the Age of a Prehistoric Burial Site," Phys.org, February 21, 2024, https://phys.org/news/2024-02-approach-carbon-dating-age-prehistoric.html (accessed January 28, 2025).

underwent significant environmental changes. But we have no proof either way—just a lot of facts that contradict uniformitarianism as ^{14}C dating models.

It's not just ^{14}C dating that is problematic. Twelve-year-old rocks from Mount St. Helens were dated as 340,000 to 2.8 million years old, using Potassium-Argon (K-Ar) testing. Once again, this dating method is based on assumptions as to how much of a particular chemical was originally present. Since there was no way to tell what the Earth was like before records were kept, faulty assumptions lead to "garbage in, garbage out" calculations.

There are many other reasons why the Earth can't be as old as secularists say. When you look at the Earth's magnetic field, it has decreased by approximately 10 percent over the last 150 years. Extrapolating backward in time to 7,000 years ago, the magnetic field would be 32 times stronger, and if we go back a million years ago, the Earth would be vaporized.[68] If the Earth were billions of years old, the amount of helium in the atmosphere would be much, much greater, and there would be much more salt in the oceans. Comets are made of ice, which means that they should only last 100,000 years at the most, yet they are still around all these years after the Big Bang.

I've barely scratched the surface here, but hopefully there's more than enough to get you reoriented. For further reading, see *The Genesis Flood* by John C. Whitcomb and Henry M. Morris, along with *The Genesis Flood Revisited* by Andrew A. Snelling.

---

68. D. Russell Humphreys, "The Mystery of Earth's Magnetic Field," Institute for Creation Research, February 1, 1989, https://www.icr.org/article/mystery-earths-magnetic-field (accessed January 30, 2025).

PART II
FILIUS

I believe in one Lord, Jesus Christ, the only-begotten Son of God, born of the Father before all ages. God from God, Light from Light, true God from true God, begotten, not made, consubstantial with the Father; through Whom all things were made. Who for us men and for our salvation came down from Heaven. And He was made flesh by the Holy Spirit from the Virgin Mary, and was made man. He was crucified for us under Pontius Pilate, suffered, and was buried. On the third day He rose again according to the Scriptures; He ascended into Heaven and sits at the right hand of the Father. He will come again in glory to judge the living and the dead, and His kingdom will have no end.

This uneducated, property-less young man has, for 2,000
years, had a greater effect on the world than all the
rulers, kings, emperors; all the conquerors, generals and
admirals, all the scholars, scientists and philosophers who
have ever lived—all of them put together. How do we
explain that—unless He really was what He said He was?

RONALD REAGAN[69]

There are plenty of discoveries validating the historical events of the Old Testament, despite the secularists' attempts to frame the events and people as myths. The discovery of the Hebrew settlement in Zanoah supports the exodus out of Egypt. In 1993, archaeologists discovered the earliest extrabiblical reference from the ninth century BC to the dynasty of King David on a carved stone slab known as the Tel Dan Stele inscription. The fragment explicitly uses the phrase "House of David." Another ninth-century BC artifact known as the Mesha Stele proclaims the victories of King Mesha of Moab over the kingdoms of Israel and Judah as well as over the House of David. Conventional secular theory holds that King David was a myth; however, these monuments validate the authenticity of the biblical King

---

69. "Ronald Reagan on the Divinity of Christ," Creation Ministries International, https://creation.com/ronald-reagan-on-the-divinity-of-christ (accessed January 31, 2025).

David. In 2009, archaeologists discovered a seal belonging to King Hezekiah, who ruled Jerusalem in the eighth century BC. The seal bears his name and iconography, verifying the king's identity and reign, which is detailed 2 Kings 18–20. In 1947, teenage Bedouin shepherds discovered large clay jars in Qumran containing what are now referred to as the Dead Sea Scrolls. These manuscripts contain Hebrew texts of every Old Testament book, with the exception of Esther, which in turn further verifies the Old Testament's historical integrity. There are numerous archeology books that provide mountains of evidence supporting the Old Testament. If you are interested in further reading, here are a few that I have found interesting: *Unearthing the Bible*, Titus Kennedy; *Exodus Found*, Frederick Baltz; and *Where God Came Down: The Archaeological Evidence*, Joel Kramer.

One of the premises for this book is to point out the evidence that validates Jesus, because He validates the Old Testament. If Jesus is who He says He is, then we can accept the Old Testament as being true. Fortunately, we don't even need the New Testament to inform us about Jesus, since there are plenty of historical references to Him outside of the Bible. In fact, Jesus is better documented than any of the other renowned figures who were His contemporaries or lived earlier. Within 150 years of His death, we know of more than forty references to Jesus outside of the Bible. For Tiberius we have ten, and for Hannibal or Alexander the Great we have none. Some of the writers were Christians, such as Clement of Rome, Ignatius of Antioch, and Justin Martyr, while others, such as Tacitus, Thallus, Josephus, Suetonius, and Pliny the Younger, were not.[70] While these extrabiblical sources clearly lend credence to the Bible, the Bible can stand

---

70. "Historicity of Jesus," New World Encyclopedia, https://www.newworldencyclopedia.org/entry/Historicity_of_Jesus (accessed January 28, 2025).

on its own, because it is different from other religious texts in that not only does it contain theological beliefs, but it is also a highly accurate record of historical events. As I've pointed out in the previous chapter, there are lots of different perspectives regarding the interpretations of the data within the natural sciences. This conflict is even more robust when interpreting history. The same skeptical approach should be taken whereby one should test the data relating to the historical record against the Bible whenever possible. Because there are strong consistencies between the two, we can have the confidence that the Bible fills in the blanks where the historical record is otherwise missing or incomplete. As such, when the Bible accurately records facts unrelated to dogma, it can be deemed credible, which in turn lends credence to dogmatic matters.

During Jesus' life, Augustus, Herod the Great, Tiberius, and Herod Antipas were some of the most renowned people in the world. No one questions that they were all real people whose lives the Bible depicts as intersecting with that of Jesus. There are so many consistencies between what was occurring during Jesus' life as described in the New Testament and what was concurrently being reflected in the generally accepted historical record that no serious person with any sense of history doubts Jesus as a historical figure. There are cocksures who claim the Gospels were originally anonymous works that were developed over time in an effort to create a mythology or legend around Jesus. But all of the earliest copies that have survived were attributed to Matthew, Mark, Luke, and John, who were either companions of Jesus or companions of His companions. For an excellent account on the history of the Gospels, see Brant Pitre's *The Case for Jesus*. Since we know He existed, once again one must consider the seminal question aptly posed by C.S. Lewis: was He Lord, lunatic, or liar?

I am awestruck when I think of the life Jesus lived. He was a man of pure goodness who only used His infinite powers to help others, never for personal gain or pleasure. No one else has ever lived that way. The New Testament provides a decent general timeline of Jesus' life, but it lacks a highly granular level of detail because His early life was without a lot of fanfare that would be noted by contemporaries, thus making it difficult to put exact dates to events. A major challenge we have with confirming ancient timelines is that the various calendars and dating systems used were not standardized across cultures. In some cultures, dates were tied to the reigns of rulers and are usually not definitive. Furthermore, the events of His birth and early life were only realized to be so important in hindsight after His death and resurrection, so the references to events are more general in nature.

However, as great as His life was, it is His resurrection that proves He is Lord. The Apostles knew this, and as witnesses, they were quick to point out that without His resurrection, Jesus would have been just another lunatic or liar (1 Corinthians 15:12). The events leading to His death and resurrection were recorded contemporaneously in much greater detail because the gravity of these events naturally resulted in them being recorded contemporaneously. In the timeline, I have included some non-verifiable dates that are conjecture but make sense because of otherwise verifiable data. While some of the specific dates I use may be conjecture, remember that these are inferences relating to very specific details contained within a verified historical record. As I continue to reiterate, there are many things we just don't know because events weren't recorded, but I do not see my use of conjecture as undermining in any way my main argument that He is who He says He is. Don't be distracted because we can't say with 100 percent certainty what the exact days and times were for some of these events; rather, once again keep in mind the big picture facts that we know are true: He was born, He died, and unlike anyone else, He was resurrected under His own power, and thus He is Lord.

August 19, 3 BC. The beginning of the forty-first year of Augustus's reign, dating from the date he was first elected consul. There were multiple significant astrological events occurring around this time that appeared to hail Augustus's stature as a divinely appointed ruler of a favored empire. These planetary conjunctions seemed to be signals that 2 BC was going to be a remarkable year for the empire, which would be celebrating the 750th anniversary of the founding of Rome and Augustus's Silver Jubilee of twenty-five years, from the time the Senate named him Augustus and Princeps. However, once you begin to see things as God does and not as man does, you can marvel at the plot twist.

September 11, 3 BC. *Conjecture:* Some speculate this was His conception, but there are a lot of coincidences that would suggest this was the day Jesus was born (see Richard Racy's *Nativity*). This was the Jewish New Year, the Feast of Trumpets, and Rosh Hashanah. Many Jewish people would be visiting Jerusalem for the holy days. The occasion of the holy days was probably also being used to enroll for a loyalty oath that would be part of the celebration of Augustus's Silver Jubilee (Luke 2). The population influx is likely why there was no room in the house where the Holy Family was staying in Bethlehem (Luke 2). This is also Noah's birthday and the day he left the ark after the Flood. Another fascinating fact is that John's celestial vision (Revelation 12:1) of a woman clothed in the sun who is giving birth matches perfectly with the alignment of the stars, Sun, and Moon on that day.

Writing in the third century AD, Irenaeus and Tertullian both note that Jesus was born in the forty-first year of Augustus's reign.

September 19, 3 BC. *Conjecture:* Jesus is circumcised. In accordance with Jewish custom, Jesus was circumcised when He was eight days old (Luke 2:21), which occurred on Yom Kippur, the Day of Atonement.

October 21, 3 BC. *Conjecture:* Jesus is presented in the temple. In accordance with Jewish custom, Jesus was presented in the temple when He was forty days old. This was witnessed by Simeon and the priestess Anna (Luke 2:34–38).

February 5, 2 BC. Augustus receives the title *Pater Patriae.* He would later write, "In my thirteenth consulship [2 BC] the Senate and the equestrian orders and the entire Roman people gave me the title of father of my Country."[71] People across the most powerful empire to have ever existed looked to Augustus as their father. Meanwhile, many miles from Rome, in the little town of Bethlehem, the one true Father had already given His Son to save us.

December 25, 2 BC. *Conjecture:* The Magi saw the series of planetary conjunctions and signs in the sky and came to a different conclusion than the Romans, because they were no doubt familiar with the Old Testament prophesies in Isaiah (7:14) and Micah (5:2). At some point they had seen enough to know it was time to head to Judea (Matthew 2). They followed the path of Jupiter, which was known as the king planet. On December 25, 2 BC, Jupiter went into retrograde

---

71. Augustus, *RES GESTAE DIVI AUGUSTI*, 35, Livius.org, https://www.livius.org/sources/content/augustus-res-gestae/ (accessed January 30, 2025).

and appeared to stop over Bethlehem. The Holy Family most likely stayed in the Bethlehem-Ephrathah area after Jesus' birth, perhaps with Zechariah, Elizabeth, and their son, John, whom Mary had visited after the Annunciation (Luke 1). When the Magi arrived, they presented gifts to the fifteen-month-old Jesus, marking the first Christmas. When the Magi decided not to report back to Herod the Great, he was enraged and ordered the Massacre of the Innocents (Matthew 2:16). All of the boys in the area under the age of two were killed, because the Magi had told Herod how long they had been tracking the celestial events. The Holy Family headed to Egypt. Their return trip to Nazareth would fulfill the prophecy in Hosea (11:1).

August 19, AD 14. Augustus dies, and thus begins Tiberius's reign, which was affirmed when the Roman Senate granted Tiberius the title of Princeps on September 17, AD 14.

Nazareth (John 19:19). In 2009, archaeologists found the remains of a house[72] in Nazareth from the first century AD, thereby refuting the skeptics who claim that Jesus of Nazareth was a myth because Nazareth was not inhabited during Jesus' life.

Capernaum by the Sea of Galilee (Mark 1:21). After being rejected as a prophet in His hometown of Nazareth, Jesus lived in Capernaum. In 1838, American Edward Robinson identified Capernaum's location, including the synagogue where Jesus taught.[73]

---

72. Diaa Hadid, "First Jesus-Era House Discovered in Nazareth," Phys.org, December 21, 2009, https://phys.org/news/2009-12-jesus-era-house-nazareth.html#google_vignette (accessed January 28, 2025).

73. Titus Kennedy, "Capernaum," Drive Thru History, July 14, 2020, https://drivethruhistory.com/capernaum/ (accessed January 28, 2025).

Pool of Bethesda near the Sheep Gate (John 5:2). The Sheep Gate, which is also referenced in the Book of Nehemiah, is next to the Pool of Bethesda, where Jesus healed a paralyzed man. The pool was discovered in the nineteenth century.[74]

Pool of Siloam (John 9:1, *et al.*). It was at this pool where a blind man regained his sight after Jesus commanded him to wash the mud that He had put on the blind man's eyes. The pool was found in 2005.[75]

Pontius Pilate (John 19:21, *et al.*). Pilate held office from AD 26 to AD 36. In 1961, Italian archaeologist Maria Teresa Fortuna discovered a limestone block bearing the inscription "Pontius Pilate, Prefect of Judea" while excavating Herod's palace near Bethlehem.[76] A ring with Pilate's name engraved on it was later discovered at the site.[77] These discoveries authenticate the accounts in the Gospels of Pilate's role in Judea at the time of Jesus and memorialize the only person outside of the Holy Trinity and the Virgin Mary who is mentioned in the Nicene Creed.

---

74. "Discovery of the Pool of Bethesda," *New Zealand Herald*, vol. 25, issue 9232 (December 8, 1888): 2, https://paperspast.natlib.govt.nz/newspapers/NZH18881208.2.64.21 (accessed January 28, 2025).

75. Thomas H. Maugh II, "Biblical Pool Discovered in Jerusalem," *Los Angeles Times*, August 9, 2005, https://www.latimes.com/archives/la-xpm-2005-aug-09-sci-siloam9-story.html (accessed January 28, 2025).

76. "Pilate Record Found; Stone with Name Is Reported in Ruin in Israel," *The New York Times*, June 19, 1961, https://www.nytimes.com/1961/06/19/archives/pilate-record-found-stone-with-name-is-reported-in-ruin-in-israel.html (accessed January 28, 2025).

77. Palko Karasz, "Pontius Pilate's Name Found in 2000-Year-Old Ring," *The New York Times*, November 30, 2018, https://www.nytimes.com/2018/11/30/world/middleeast/pontius-pilate-ring.html (accessed January 28, 2025).

Caiaphas (Matthew 26:3, *et al.*). In 1990, a highly decorated ossuary[78] was discovered with the inscription "Joseph bar Caiaphas." The location and detail of the ossuary are consistent with it containing the remains of the Jewish high priest who presided over the trial of Jesus, according to the Gospels. A nearby ossuary contained a coin minted by Herod Agrippa (AD 37–44), thereby further dating the artifacts.

April 3, AD 33 (14 Nissan). *Conjecture:* All four Gospels (Matthew 27, *et al.*) provide subtle yet substantial clues as to when the crucifixion occurred, since they all record Jesus' crucifixion occurring shortly before evening on the day before the Sabbath (Saturday), when Passover was celebrated on the Sabbath. April 3, AD 33, was one such Friday that preceded Passover occurring on a Saturday.

The Gospels record that the midday sky was darkened and a massive earthquake shook the area. The Greek writer Phlegon, who was born around AD 80, was quoted as writing that in the 202nd Olympiad (July 1, AD 32, to June 30, AD 3), the sun went dark at the sixth hour, turning day into night, and an earthquake in Bithynia (Turkey) toppled many buildings. Julius Africanus, a third-century AD historian, quoted Thallus, a historian in the first century AD, regarding Jesus' crucifixion and noted a terrible midday darkening of the sky and a massive earthquake in Judea. In 2012, archeologists confirmed through core samples on the western shore of the Dead Sea that a massive earthquake occurred in the area between AD 26 and 36.[79]

---

78. Dr. Catherine Murphy, "Caiaphas Ossuary," Santa Clara University Religious Studies Department, https://webpages.scu.edu/ftp/cmurphy/courses/sctr027/artifacts/caiaphas-ossuary.htm (accessed January 28, 2025).

79. Jefferson Williams, Markus J. Schwab, and Achim Brauer, "An Early First-Century Earthquake in the Dead Sea," *International Geology Review*, vol. 54, no. 10 (July 2012):1219–28, https://www.researchgate.net/publication/229810979_An_early_first-century_earthquake_in_the_Dead_Sea (accessed January 28, 2025).

On the day of the crucifixion, the Gospels also refer to a blood Moon (that is, an eclipse causing a reddish-colored moon). Sunset marks the beginning of Passover. Modern astronomy software can show us that on April 3 around 6:20 p.m., as the Sun was setting in Jerusalem, the Moon was rising. Observers would have been expecting a full yellow moon, but instead they would have seen the Moon rising in eclipse, with a blood-red hue, and with its upper portion blotted out (Acts 2:20). But that's not all. Once again, perspective adds to the story. If the alignment of the Earth, Moon, and Sun was viewed from the Moon, the Earth would be seen as blotting out the Sun. If you then looked at the bigger picture in the heavens, you would have the Sun blotted out in the heart of Aries the Ram. Cocksures see just another cosmic coincidence. I see the work of the Creator who offered up the Lamb of God to take away the sins of the world, not unlike when He provided His faithful and steadfast servant Abraham a ram to sacrifice in the stead of his son Isaac, a sacrifice that would seal God's covenant with the Jewish people (Genesis 22:13).

Church of the Holy Sepulchre. The historian Eusebius wrote in the fourth century AD that the emperor Hadrian had built a temple to Venus in the second century AD over the tomb of Jesus. Eusebius's contemporary, Jerome, recorded that Constantine built the Church of the Holy Sepulchre over the same site, which survives today, albeit having been rebuilt several times. Witnesses provided firsthand accounts of the empty tomb, thereby supporting the claim that Jesus was resurrected from the dead. While nonbelievers may discount this evidence, the fact that Pontius Pilate had the tomb sealed and guarded adds credence to the witness accounts.

St. Peter's Basilica (Matthew 16:18). Jesus' resurrection is further supported by the many people who saw Jesus after He arose (Luke 24:13–49; 1 Corinthians 15:7; and others). I see the most important contemporary evidence of His resurrection to be the change that occurred within His Apostles. Just a few days earlier, Peter was denying that he even knew Jesus, and after the Resurrection, Peter was willing to suffer the most violent painful death imaginable. Only seeing the resurrected Jesus could have had this dramatic of an effect on Peter. After his crucifixion circa AD 64–66, St. Peter was buried outside the city walls on Vatican Hill. Around AD 326, the construction of St. Peter's Basilica began, with workers using millions of tons of fill to level the foundation that was built on top of the necropolis that had grown around St. Peter's burial site. The original basilica as well as the current basilica, on which rebuilding began in 1506, were centered over St. Peter's grave, thereby fulfilling the literal words of Jesus, which had already been fulfilled figuratively.[80]

Shroud of Turin. Now for the *pièce de résistance*. The Shroud of Turin is the most important historical artifact for Christianity, bar none, because in it we have physical proof of Jesus and His Resurrection. Once again, the genius of God is on display. He has provided us with all the proof we need to know that Jesus is who He said He is. Like Jesus Himself, the Shroud is either real or a fake. There is overwhelming evidence as to its authenticity, yet the cocksures refuse to accept it, in part because of "settled science," mainly in the form of the 1988 ^{14}C dating test showing the Shroud to be "unequivocally" dated from AD 1260–1390. God sets an interesting intellectual trap

---

80. See John O'Neill's *The Fisherman's Tomb* for the fascinating details of the history of St. Peters Basilica.

for cocksures. Believing that the Shroud is a fake requires an incredible amount of faith in the unknown and the unexplainable, since there is no "settled science" that can determine how it was made.[81] Yet there it is, a virtual Polaroid of His being and Resurrection. I can't help but think of Jesus telling the story of Lazarus and the rich man (Dives). In the parable, Dives pleads that Lazarus be sent to warn Dives's family about his fate in Hell, but Abraham reminds Dives that no matter what, some people will never believe (Luke 16:19–31). The intellectual trap set by the Shroud must be particularly unsettling for cocksures because as technology advances, the Shroud's authenticity becomes more unimpeachable, since the images and data contained on it continue to confirm the Shroud to be nothing short of miraculous.

The Shroud is a linen cloth measuring 8 cubits by 2 cubits (approximately 14 feet long by 3.5 feet wide) that contains highly detailed front and back images of a man who was crucified. The size of the Shroud is consistent with the units of measurements used in the first century. It has the unique three-to-one herringbone twill pattern, which is similar to cloth discovered at Masada (dated between 40 BC and AD 73). The Shroud was made from flax grown in the western Levant (Israel, Lebanon, Jordan, and Syria).[82] It would have been an expensive cloth at the time (Matthew 27:57–61, *et al.*). The Shroud as it is presently known has a documented history that dates

---

81. The Shroud of Turin Research Project (STURP) 1981 report states, "There are no chemical or physical methods known which can account for the totality of the image, nor can any combination of physical, chemical, biological, or medical circumstances explain the image adequately." From "A Summary of STURP's Conclusions," Shroud of Turin Website, https://www.shroud.com/78conclu.htm (accessed January 28, 2025).

82. Giulio Fanti, "Analysis of Ancient Fabrics, Example of the Holy Shroud in Turin," *World Scientific News* 189 (2024): 236–57, https://worldscientificnews.com/wp-content/uploads/2024/01/WSN-189-2024-236-257-1.pdf (accessed January 29, 2025).

from the 1350s; however, it is most likely the same cloth known as the Image of Edessa and later the Mandylion that was documented as healing King Abgar of Edessa, who ruled at the time of the Resurrection. While the Bible does not provide a description of what Jesus looked like, it is obvious by looking at the facial features of the Shroud, and art historians confirm as much, that the Shroud became the basis for His traditional image long before the thirteenth century. The wounds directly correspond, in amazing detail, to the description of the wounds Jesus incurred on the day He was crucified (a crown of thorns, spear wound to the chest, pierced wrists, flagellum marks, and so on). The image is not made from paint, pigmentation, or dye; rather, the yellow-sepia discoloration is from the oxidation and dehydration of the cellulose in certain individual strands of the outermost fibrils of the Shroud's fibers, which are a fraction of the diameter of a human hair.[83] Jesus' feet marks have dirt containing travertine aragonite, which is a rare calciferous mineral only known to be found near Jerusalem. The Shroud contains pollen particles from plants that blossomed in the Jerusalem area during March and April. There are wounds that can only be seen with the aid of photographic instruments and microscopes, which weren't invented until hundreds of years after the Shroud's supposed date. Bloodstains from the head region can be distinguished as coming separately from veins and arteries, knowledge of which would be unknown to an artist in the Middle Ages. The nail wounds in the wrist and the resulting severance of the median nerve are medically accurate to an advanced degree and counter to the conventional

---

83. Giovanni Fazio and Francesca Riotto, "About the Shroud Body Image," *Open Journal of Social Sciences* 12 (2024): 25–31, http://info.submit4journal.com/id/eprint/3380/1/jss_2024010914260252.pdf (accessed January 29, 2025).

wisdom of Jesus being nailed in the palms. The blood on the Shroud is type AB, which interestingly, is the same blood type that appears on the Sudarium of Oviedo.[84] The Sudarium of Oviedo appears to be a cloth that was wrapped around Jesus' head at some point. The bloodstains from Jesus' wounds on the Sudarium and the Shroud match up closely, and the fact that the rarest human blood type appears on both supports their interrelation.[85]

I won't go into much further detail, since there is an extraordinary amount of literature with many more fascinating details regarding the Shroud.[86] Because it's obvious that the Shroud is real, I am not going to waste your time here debunking the claims that the Shroud is a fake. Cocksures are going to cocksure. If you want the rebuttals, they exist and you can find them in all of these resources, including the many reasons why the 1988 ^{14}C tests dating the Shroud to AD 1260–1390 were not reliable. These resources also go into detail as to how other dating methods, such as the "Wide-Angle X-ray Scattering" method, produced results that the Shroud is approximately two thousand years old. The bonus fact to remember is that because there were so many eyewitnesses and so much other evidence, we don't need the Shroud to be real for Jesus to be who He says He is. If the Shroud were found to be a forgery, it would then just be an amazing piece of art to remind us of what He did for us, not unlike Michaelangelo's *La Pietà*.

---

84. The AB blood type is also present in the Holy Tunic of Argenteuil and certain Eucharistic miracles. For a fascinating analysis of bio-theology see *A Cardiologist Examines Jesus*, by Dr. Franco Serafini.

85. C. Barta, R. Álvarez, A. Ordóñez, A. Sánchez, and J. García, "New coincidences between Shroud of Turin and Sudarium of Oviedo," https://doi.org/10.1051/shsconf/20151500008 (accessed March 23, 2025).

86. See Mark Antonacci's *Test the Shroud*, Joe Marino's *The 1988 C-14 Dating of the Shroud of Turin*, and the movie *Who Can He Be?*

I like this synopsis of the evidence by Martin Haigh:

> Whereas an artist can copy an existing negative, he cannot imagine it before it exists. How could an artist create, on a flat surface the back and front of a crucified man so accurately that from it a computer can now produce the three-dimensional figure that must have been contained in the Shroud? If the image was made simply by direct contact then, when the cloth was stretched out flat, the image would not be anatomically accurate; the face, for example, would be almost half as wide again as a normal face. The material of the Shroud is, in fact, a comparatively thick herring-bone weave and would stand away from the body by as much as 2 to 3 centimeters in some places. However the image was made, in other words, it was not made simply by the transference onto the cloth of the perspiration, dirt, dust and blood on the crucified body. How could the forger have guessed so many anatomical and medical details, as for example the blood-stains, with such accuracy at a time when detailed knowledge of that kind was unknown? After years of exhaustive testing, the scientists are no nearer establishing how the image was created.[87]

I would like to offer some conjecture as to what happened at the moment of the Resurrection. We know from various accounts in the Gospels that Jesus regularly dematerialized after the Resurrection (John 20:19). The images on the Shroud, unlike a typical painting, appear as photographic negatives. Note that photography wasn't

---

87. Martin Haigh, "The Shroud Defended," *The Tablet* 3 (December 1988): 1392–93.

invented until hundreds of years after the cocksures' dating of the Shroud. The appearance of the images as negatives is one of the factors that leads to the best hypothesis we have today: that the images were formed by a burst of radiation emanating from Jesus as He dematerialized. The visibility of Jesus' bones and teeth is consistent with this theory. The massive burst of radiation emanating from within Him while His body was levitating resulted in the three-dimensional nature of the images and left the Shroud to collapse onto itself with no flattening of the image as He dematerialized.[88] This would explain why the bloody areas on the Shroud were not stuck to His body, nor were they smeared as would be expected if the Shroud were pulled off of Him (picture what a bandage looks like when you pull it off). The Shroud also offers a glimpse into the future, because when He returns it will be in a flash of light—just like His Resurrection which was documented on the Shroud (Luke 17:24; Matthew 24:27).

There's an AI-generated image of Jesus[89] from the Shroud that is interesting, but if you need help comprehending all that is memorialized in the Shroud, I suggest checking out "The Mystery Man" exhibition by curator Álvaro Blanco.[90] I don't know how anyone cannot be humbled when they see this portrayal of Jesus and know what He suffered for each of us. But once again, it shouldn't surprise us that some remain indifferent, because He told us that "You will be ever hearing but never understanding; you will be ever seeing but never

---

88. Dr. Gilbert Lavoi, *The Shroud of Jesus: And the Sign John Ingeniously Concealed* (Nashua, NH: Sophia Institute Press, 2023).

89. Pablo Kay, "Is That Really What Jesus Looked Like? Experts Weigh In on Sensational AI Image," Angelus News, August 23, 2024, https://angelusnews.com/arts-culture/ai-jesus-shroud-turin/ (accessed January 29, 2025).

90. Filipe D'Avillez, "Behind 'The Mystery Man' and the Shroud of Turin," The Pillar, October 17, 2022, https://www.pillarcatholic.com/p/behind-the-mystery-man-the-turin-shroud-as-youve-never-seen-it-before (accessed January 29, 2025).

perceiving" (Matthew 13:14 NIV). Keep the Shroud or this exhibit in mind the next time you hear a cocksure scoffing at God, questioning why He has done this or hasn't done that, or asking why there is suffering in the world. We aren't able to think as He does, but we do know that while we may encounter suffering, He has suffered more despite the fact that He was sinless, unlike us. We can also take comfort in knowing that He has a reason for everything, and if we simply believe in Him, we will have eternal life (John 6:47).

PART III

SPIRITUS SANCTUS

I believe in the Holy Spirit, the Lord and giver of life, Who proceeds from the Father and the Son. Who, with the Father and the Son, is adored and glorified: Who has spoken through the Prophets.

The Spirit is the first power we practically experience,
but the last power we come to understand.

OSWALD CHAMBERS

Even after considering all of the scientific and historical evidence in this book supporting the God of the Bible, there is no doubt that there are still readers who believe that they sit here today as the material end product of a single cell that long ago fantastically emerged from some primordial soup, amazingly learned to replicate, and methodically evolved over eons into the person they are today. Okay, sure they did. But to those folks I have to ask: How did they, or one of their ancestors, first become conscious? With a hat tip to Aristotle, I would ask them what they think rocks dream about, or if rocks are conscious. If not, why, since rocks have been around longer than humans? Lastly, I would ask if they believe that *Pinocchio* and *Ted* are true stories.

The scientific and historical evidence for the existence of God is overwhelming, but it is the spiritual dimension that in some respects is the most convincing, because it is self-evident through the ordinary human experience regardless of one's access to the scientific or historical evidence. The human experience is such that we *all* have this innate intuition that we are connected to something outside ourselves from somewhere within ourselves. This is the Holy Spirit in action, not some evolutionary by-product. If this sense is the product of an element of survival but is false, why would it survive?

To understand how the spiritual dimension is self-evident, we have to appreciate the concept of "self." Our sense of self is entrenched in our consciousness. Human consciousness is based and rooted in first-person perspectives. First-person perspectives are what substantiate a person's self-consciousness. I am a conscious being because I can perceive things, and *I know that I can perceive things.* Consciousness is much more complicated than merely reacting to stimuli. I can observe the physical qualities that make you *you*, but I will never know what it is like to be you or why there are certain things that you like and dislike. However, I do know what it is like to be me, and I know the things I like and dislike. Moreover, you and I can share real and imaginary experiences, which is only possible because we are both conscious. Think of a joke. It exists only in your mind, yet when you tell me the joke, you are expressing something that has only existed as an immaterial by-product of your mind, yet it has the ability to elicit a physical reaction in me. One person might think the joke is funny, while another person might have no reaction. There was nothing material about the joke other than the response. If there was never anything material about that joke, it cannot have a material origin, so it must have originated in the immaterial or spiritual realm that is being accessed by a material connection. Consciousness allows us to make that connection between the immaterial and material realms.

Consciousness is not of the material realm, so where could

consciousness possibly come from if not from God, who exists across realms? We have consciousness because we are the product of a Creator who wants to communicate with us. While only humans have the gift to manifest our thoughts through speech, writing, and actions, it is through our spirit, which is a faculty or capacity, of our soul, that we can communicate with God. Have you ever thought about what language you think in? You don't need to think in a language to communicate with God. Our minds and our souls are private and are designed as such so that, unlike our actions, no one can truly know the complete you but God. Our minds enable us to use the gift of prayer to individually express ourselves to our Creator. He wants us to use the gift of consciousness to seek Him so that we may do His will. The Holy Spirit communicates with our souls, dispensing the truth and God's will. If we ignore the Holy Spirit, we open the door to evil spirits. Whether we communicate and act on the guidance of the Holy Spirit or evil spirits (1 Timothy 4:1) ultimately impacts our souls.

Consciousness in turn allows for conscience. Conscience is the manifestation of the soul and drives our choices. Our choices impact our bodies and our souls, which is why we can feel pain and pleasure on a physical and spiritual level. Materialists say we are nothing more than slabs of meat, with our brains being merely a particular cut of meat in which neurons randomly fire to create the thoughts that pop into our heads. If that were the case, how could anyone trust any of their own thoughts if they were just random chemical reactions? I know that the slab of meat I see in the mirror is only part of who I am. While our eyes respond to light waves and our ears to sound waves, what are our consciences responding to? If I were to get a heart transplant, I wouldn't become a different person. Our bodies change over time, but that is not what dictates the changes to who we become over time. The body is the container for the soul, and it is this combination of our physical and immaterial nature that prompted George MacDonald to advise, "Never tell a child 'You have a soul.' Teach him, you are a soul; you have a body."[91] Our sinful nature coincides with the fact that our bodies are weak and corruptible (Matthew 26:41). Repetitive pain can harden our bodies with callouses and our souls with indifference or evil. Indifference or evil in our souls opens the door for us to do evil with our bodies. Evil and sins of the flesh can damage our souls. This is also why Jesus warned us that it is from within a person's heart that we become defiled (Mark 7:20; Matthew 15:18). He also warned us to fear those who can kill the soul, not the body (Matthew 10:28). Fortunately, we can train our souls to contravene what our bodies want to do, and it is through our belief in God and accessing the Holy Spirit that we can save our souls.

Not so! At least according to the materialists who claim that we don't have free will. The cocksures tell us that we don't have free will because spikes in brain activity can be observed prior to our conscious awareness of making a decision. However, it is the soul, not the brain, that enables consciousness. Our brains process the inputs we receive through our senses, which our bodies experience in the physical three-dimensional world. Consciousness is not computational; it is relational to our quest for meaning and purpose. Materialistic processors like computers or brains don't care about meanings, only computations. Thoughts and meanings are immaterial, and while they can be represented on computational machines, they can only be created in the mind, because intellect is not found in the brain; it

---

91. George MacDonald, "Quotable Quote," Goodreads, https://www.goodreads.com/quotes/8131121-never-tell-a-child-you-have-a-soul-teach-him (accessed January 30, 2025).

is immaterial. We know this because the brain can be split, but the mind cannot. Benjamin Libet undermined the materialist claim of our lack of free will with the concept of "free won't."[92] Libet's observations enabled him to conclude what we all intuitively know, because we all have shared experiences of being bombarded with preconscious and unconscious motives and stimulations. Although we may not want to admit it at times, in our souls we all know that we are freely capable to comply or not comply with those motives and stimulations. Libet observed that these decisions to comply or not comply are not generated in the brain and therefore are not of materialistic origin. If this sounds familiar, it's because this exactly parallels the concept of original sin. Our corruptible bodies and souls are burdened with motives that are beyond our control, yet our souls can override those motives. Ask yourself: Who am I? Am I a product of my actions or my impulses? You are the product of your decisions and actions, and as C.S. Lewis noted, "Good and evil both increase at compound interest. That is why the little decisions you and I make every day are of such infinite importance."[93]

If someone doesn't believe in free will, then it makes no sense to pay attention to the randomly generated gibberish from a slab of meat who believes in a blind watchmaker who is incapable of freely deciding whether to pick his nose or wind his watch. Without free will, the materialist is no more than a product of randomness. Interestingly, the reason why AI will never achieve consciousness is because it cannot create randomness or true choice; it is always the servant to its master, that is, the programmer. On the other hand,

92. Benjamin Libet, "Can Conscious Experience Affect Brain Activity?" *Journal of Consciousness Studies*, vol. 10, no.12 (2003): 24–28.

93. C.S. Lewis, "Quotable Quote," Goodreads, https://www.goodreads.com/quotes/537819-good-and-evil-both-increase-at-compound-interest-that-is (accessed January 30, 2025).

the rational person knows we have free will because they know that we process information. We can create random outcomes. We can observe, research, and come to rational conclusions while rejecting false claims. We can acknowledge our mistakes and choose to fix them. We can sin, but we can also repent. While stupid people don't have the capacity to realize they are stupid, the free will denier absolutely has the capacity to know they have a soul and free will, but they kick, scratch, and scream to deny it, because to admit it would trigger implications that they would prefer to leave buried under a pile of doubt and misdirection.

If your birth was an accident and your death is an accident, then your life is meaningless. Full stop. Fortunately, that is not the case because God has a plan for each of us, and that is why He ensouls us. Jesus told His disciples that the Holy Spirit would guide them to the truth (John 16:13). The Holy Spirit teaches us from within; this is why we are all familiar with the expression "gut feelings." If you examine the cardinal virtues (prudence, justice, fortitude, and temperance) and the cardinal sins (pride, lust, envy, wrath, greed, gluttony, and sloth), what they have in common is that they are all immaterial concepts that only have real-world implications when we act on them. They are like math in this sense. And like math, virtues and sin must come from nonmaterial sources—God and Satan. But unlike math, you don't need the erudition of mathematicians to understand virtue and sin because they are self-evident to everyone who has a gut.

So then, what or where is this immaterial realm that our minds and souls are interfacing with, and how do we interact with it after death? Once again, this is more of the *invisible* created by God and referenced in the Nicene Creed. Because our bodies are confined to a three-dimensional world, we cannot comprehend a fourth dimension, any more than a third dimension can be comprehended from a two-dimensional world. Materialists will agree that there is no reason not to believe that additional dimensions exist.[94, 95] As such, the important implication is that our three-dimensional world could be contained within a four-dimensional world, which could be contained within a five-dimensional world, and so on. Cocksures like to point their telescopes into the heavens and mockingly ask why they can never see the Flying Spaghetti Monster, Heaven, or Hell. But space is not the final frontier, and time is not a separate dimension, since it operates across all three spatial dimensions. God exists outside of time as we know it (2 Peter 3:8; Psalm 90:4), and although we can't be certain, He is most likely in one or more of these higher dimensions. When Jesus died on the cross, He gave up His Spirit (John 19:30) and went to paradise (Luke 23:42). The Shroud of Turin provides physical evidence that Jesus dematerialized. His resurrected body and Spirit were then reunited. After His death, the Gospels record several instances of Jesus appearing out of thin air and then once again dematerializing (John 20:11–29). During the Transfiguration, Jesus apparently changed form at the same time that Moses and Elijah amazingly appeared out of nowhere to Peter and the other disciples (Matthew 17:4). Jesus provided additional insight into the possibility of multiple dimensions when He told the story of a poor beggar named Lazarus and a rich man (Dives). When both men died, Lazarus could see that Dives was in Hell, and there was a great chasm between them that neither could cross (Luke 16:19–31). We can't be exactly certain what awaits us, but we can be certain that something does.

94. Carl Sagan, "Cosmos—Carl Sagan—4th Dimension," YouTube, March 24, 2009, https://www.youtube.com/watch?v=UnURElCzGc0 (accessed January 29, 2025).

95. xkcdHatGuy, "4th Dimension Explained by a High School Student," YouTube, January 5, 2010, https://www.youtube.com/watch?v=eGguwYPC32I (accessed January 29, 2025).

The evidence supporting our intuition that God is with us in a spiritual realm that we are connected to via our souls is so obvious that Pascal concluded, "There is a God-shaped vacuum in the heart of each man which cannot be satisfied by any created thing but only by God the Creator, made known through Jesus Christ." That is the real God of the gaps. Fortunately, so long as we believe in Him, the Holy Spirit will fill that gap. The importance of this powerful connection between God and man reinforces the importance of the Holy Spirit to the Trinity. The innateness of being able to connect directly to God through the Holy Spirit makes it self-authenticating, and those who teach otherwise ought to proceed with caution. While Jesus was usually abundant in offering forgiveness, He seemed particularly stern about protecting children (Luke 17:2) and defending the Holy Spirit, so listen carefully when He says, "But whoever blasphemes against the Holy Spirit will never have forgiveness but is guilty of an everlasting sin" (Mark 3:29; cf. Matthew 12:30).

PART IV

PRACTICUM

I believe in one holy,
catholic and apostolic
Church. I confess one baptism
for the remission of sins. And
I look for the resurrection
of the dead, and the life
of the age to come. Amen.

God has provided enough evidence in this life to convince anyone willing to believe, yet He has also left some ambiguity so as not to compel the unwilling. In this way, God gives us the opportunity to either love Him or to reject Him without violating our freedom.

NORMAN GEISLER

M y main purpose for writing this book was to provide the answers to *why* I believe in God and *what* I believe, which was decreed by the Council of Nicaea 1,700 years ago. Hopefully, you find the evidence as compelling as I do for the existence of the triune God of the Bible. The evidence is so overwhelming to me that I often fear being on the wrong side of God, because "He will come again in glory to judge the living and the dead, and His kingdom will have no end." Heaven and Hell are real, and Jesus was clear about the angels separating the wicked from the righteous and throwing the wicked into a fiery furnace (Matthew 13). I have just enough wisdom to know that I don't want to be burned for eternity in a fiery furnace. I regularly imagine what it will be like to stand before Him, and I wonder if some sort of a jury of my peers would make a finding that I was a Christian or not. Scoffers say they can't believe in a

God who wants us to fear Him, but clearly, He does, and He tells us that fear of the Lord is the beginning of wisdom (Proverbs 9:10). Fear of the Lord is the beginning of wisdom, not a ticket to Heaven. Believing in Jesus is the ticket. But what does it mean to be a believer? Flawed people attempting to put their beliefs into practice has been the challenge for millennia. I don't pretend to have the answers, just some observations.

While we each are offered a one-to-one relationship with God, it seems clear that He also wants us to accept the Holy Spirit and share the faith with others (Matthew 28:19–20) so that we come together as one holy, catholic (note that the small *c* in *catholic* denotes "universal") and apostolic Church that effectuates His will. Jesus created a Church first and told Peter that he was going to be the rock on which Jesus built it. The Apostles were sent to spread the Gospel before Jesus was crucified (Matthew 10), which indicates that Jesus was satisfied with their understanding of His message and their ability to deliver it effectively. There were always going to be questions to which believers needed answers, and there was no Bible to look to because it wasn't finished being compiled until the fourth century. This is one of the reasons that the *sola scriptura* argument never made much sense to me—there need to be some authority figures within the Church to resolve doctrinal issues. Differences of opinion on various matters within the Church were there from the outset. Mark seemed to have had some sort of a falling out with Paul at one point (Acts 15:36–39), and there was a significant disagreement early on amongst the Apostles over the requirements for believers to be circumcised. The solution to solving disagreements was to convene those who had the requisite knowledge and authority to affirm a decision. This is why the Council of Jerusalem was convened (Acts 15). The Council proved to be an effective method for answering questions and resolving disagreements.

Eventually, the lowercase *c* became a capital *C*, and the *Catholic Church* became synonymous with the Church. It was the Catholic Church that would lead ecumenical councils, which was a gathering of bishops to discuss matters of doctrine. The Council of Nicaea in AD 325 produced the Nicene Creed. After the seventh council, Nicaea II in AD 787, the Great Schism occurred, after which the Eastern Orthodox Churches stopped recognizing ecumenical councils. Once fractures started, they never stopped. Luther had ninety-five reasons to dislike the Catholic Church, so he started the Lutheran Church. Calvin didn't like the Lutheran Church, whence came the Calvinists. Henry VIII wanted a divorce, so he started the Anglican Church. It's one thing for the Catholic and Eastern Orthodox Churches to split over doctrinal matters, but my view is that it's an entirely different issue when denominations are spun off because they are devoted to their founders, because it seems like the wrong person is at the head of that church. St. Augustine summed it up well when he said, "If you believe what you like in the Gospels, and reject what you don't like, it is not the Gospel you believe, but yourself."

So what to do with so many denominations and questions of faith that are not addressed in the Creed? One would think that if the answer to a question is in red letters, then there shouldn't be too much up for debate, but even that's not the case. Moreover, there are a lot of questions not directly answered by Jesus. This is why history and tradition are important. Accumulated knowledge is one of the hallmarks of human progress and the reason Chesterton thought we shouldn't drive through a fence without asking why it was put up. Since humans are mortal, it is the institutions that help fulfill the role of transferring knowledge. The doctors of the Catholic Church played a critical role in developing Christian theology and doctrines. Moreover, it is indisputable that there have been countless members of the Catholic Church who remained true to the faith and can be universally viewed as role models. Despite all the good that has been done by the Catholic Church, an honest assessment exposes the many betrayals. Institutions fail when their caretakers are not careful and selective when searching for people who are to serve and preserve the mission of the institution. Disciples must put the institution's purposes above their own when the two are in conflict. The honorable thing is to openly state their opposition and be prepared to resign rather than surreptitiously try to change the institution. The Catholic Church was the cornerstone for Christians, but unfortunately, it became a flawed institution, resulting in its moral authority rightfully being questioned time and time again. Napoleon Bonaparte once taunted a Catholic cardinal by threatening, "Your Eminence, are you not aware that I have the power to destroy the Catholic Church?" To which the cardinal quipped, "Your Majesty, we Catholic clergy have done our best to destroy the Church for the last eighteen hundred years. We have not succeeded, and neither will you."

The good news is that we can be bothered by the failings of the Catholic Church for Christian reasons. The Catholic Church's failures have been the result of the sins committed by the *people* running the institution. The sins they have committed have been transgressions against Christian doctrines. Jesus referred to the Pharisees and the Sadducees as a brood of vipers, but He did not denigrate the Torah. Few would be surprised if upon His second coming He made the same assessment of some within the Catholic Church, and other denominations as well, for that matter. This is why it is important to look to the doctrines and not the vipers. No matter what your opinion is of the Catholic Church, its foundation and history preserve its relevance regarding doctrinal matters.

I would suggest that professing the Creed is paramount to aligning oneself with a denomination. The Christian Church ought to be viewed as a multi-object system where Creed-centered denominations are masses that rely on one another as they orbit God as the system's barycenter. At the risk of mixing metaphors, God must always be our true north, and Creed-centered denominations are a sort of magnetic north and a starting point for seeking answers. Denominations do ultimately matter, because one must be careful with one's own interpretations of matters of faith. If Jesus opined on a matter, then the plain meaning of His teaching is usually obvious. For other matters, surround yourself with truth-seekers and people who can respectfully challenge and be challenged when exchanging ideas. Recognize that there is nothing new under the Sun (Ecclesiastes 1:9), and take a look at what others within the Christian Church have to say. Also recognize that it requires humility to know that an absolute answer may not always be available in this lifetime. As far as congregating is concerned, be thoughtful about how the Eucharist is celebrated, and then ask yourself if you are attending services for a performance or for the Word? Is it the word you *want* to hear, or the Word you *need* to hear? Since we are all flawed, we should expect to be uncomfortable at times when hearing His Word, just as His disciples were.

Remember that deeds are evidence of theology. The Apostles saw someone whom they did not know doing deeds in Jesus' name. Jesus told them not to stop him because "whoever is not against us is for us" (Mark 9:38). It is important that we keep this in mind so that we bolster the Christian Church, which is epochal in helping us navigate this fallen world. It's a lie when people proclaim there is some general arc of history toward goodness. In this broken world of ours, the arc is toward chaos and evil. Cynics only want to see the bad things that have been done in the name of "religion." It's okay to acknowledge that evil has certainly been perpetuated in the name of Christianity, but evil has never been done in the practice of actual Christianity. Don't conflate the amorphous use of "religion" with the God of the Bible. It is the God of the Bible who is responsible for all that is good in the world. He established that we are created in His image (Genesis 1:26) and that we are all created equal in His eyes (Genesis 1:27). Without Christianity there would be no basis for human rights or charity (Matthew 25:35). Be grateful that it was Christians such as Newton and Galileo who were responsible for the founding of modern science and the great universities of the world, because they were driven by their faith to search for answers to bring them closer to their Creator.

Defend the Bible as being more than just a collection of dogmas. Christianity is not some abstract spirituality or philosophy. The Bible and Christianity are gifts, and they give us real-life cheat codes for a happy life. Too often, Christianity is presented as a burden. Not so. He tells us that His yoke is easy, and the burden is light (Matthew 11:30). A Christian life is not meant to be limiting; it's meant to be liberating. God wants us to be free and happy (Romans 8; Galatians 5), and the simplest way to do that is to listen to His Son with whom He is well pleased (Matthew 17:5). Sin is the result of something good being warped into something evil. God tells us how we should live our lives because He knows that we all greatly benefit by avoiding sin. He tells us that moderation and humility are necessary to avoid sin. It's okay to eat; just don't be a glutton. It's okay to have stuff; just be grateful for what you have, share your excesses, and don't take other people's things. Money is not the root of all evil; it's the *love* of money that is. It's okay to enjoy physical intimacy; just keep it between you and your spouse.

Making these arguments is not easy when the cultural gatekeepers disagree with the premise of Christianity. Sometimes all it takes is a catchy tune and vapid lyrics to legitimize a crooner's worldview and spread the misdiagnosis of a problem. For a secular singer-songwriter cynic, it's Heaven and religion that are the problems, not sin. However, with a Christian worldview, avoiding sin would solve a lot of problems. There would be no murder. No wars. The poor would be cared for. There would be no pornography, sex trafficking, or physical or sexual abuse. There would be no rape, divorce, or prostitution too. Imagine.

Putting Christianity into practice is always going to be a challenge for all of us flawed people. The parable of the workers in the vineyard is particularly instructive as to how we ought to think about what we want out of our lives. In the parable, the landowner hires workers throughout the day. At the end of the day, he ends up paying everyone the same amount. Some of the workers who started early in the day are displeased, because they feel they were treated unfairly, despite being given exactly what they agreed on. The smart-ass will snidely remark that the landowner is going to have a tough time finding workers the next morning. That is funny, but as usual with Jesus' parables, if you scratch beneath the surface, you can find the wisdom that outflanks the smart-ass. Jesus is using the parable to explain how people who accept Him later in life will be rewarded similarly to the people who have followed Him for their entire lives. This parable was a foreshadowing of the "Good Thief," known as Dismas, who, while hanging on a cross next to Jesus, asked Jesus to remember him when Jesus entered His kingdom. Jesus told Dismas that Dismas would join Him in Paradise because he was penitent and had come to believe. Anyone who thinks it is unfair that Dismas is rewarded the same as someone who followed Jesus their whole life is missing the big picture. Living a Christian life results in a full and happy life; you are not missing out on anything when you avoid sin. That doesn't mean it's easy, as C.S. Lewis observed:

> No man knows how bad he is till he has tried very hard to be good. A silly idea is current that good people do not know what temptation means. This is an obvious lie. Only those who try to resist temptation know how strong it is. After all, you find out the strength of the German army by fighting against it, not by giving in. You find out the strength of a wind by trying to walk against it, not by lying down. A man who gives in to temptation after five minutes simply does not know what it would have been like an hour later. That is why bad people, in one sense, know very little about badness—they have lived a sheltered life by always giving in. We never find out the strength of the evil impulse inside us until we try to fight it: and Christ, because He was the only man who never yielded to temptation, is also the only man who knows to the full what temptation means—the only complete realist.

The Devil is the god of everlasting death. When temptation arises, picture how disappointed you will be with yourself after sinning. Then conjure Syrio Forel and think about what it would be like to say, "*NON HODIE, SATAN. VADE RETRO!*" ("Not today, Satan. Begone!").

CONCLUSION

Truth stands the test of time; lies are soon exposed.

PROVERBS 12:19 TLB

QUOD ERAT DEMONSTRANDUM is the Latin phrase that is translated to mean "that which was to be proved." It is used at the conclusion of mathematical proofs or arguments to notate that the conclusion has been definitively proven or demonstrated. Some authors choose the abbreviation "Q.E.D.," while others have used various symbols, including a solid black square, a solid black rectangle, or sometimes a hollow square or block, which I happen the be partial to.

The Nicene Creed has stood the test of time because not only is it a profession of faith, but it is also a profession of truth.

AFTERWORD

I had originally planned to include a Frequently Asked Questions section in this book but have decided instead to maintain a Substack page. For updates, FAQs, observations, and other related items of interest please see:

WWW.CREDOINUNUMDEUM.SUBSTACK.COM